TABERNACLE WORKBOOK
Old Testament Symbolism Points to Jesus

A 12–Lesson Journey Through the Tabernacle
for Youth and Adults

by
Nancy Fisher

- Follow the High Priest and the Path of Worship

- Discover the significance of sacrifice

- See God's Plan of Redemption

- Use with the Tabernacle wall chart

What's Inside

Preview, Notes, Reference Guide, Diagram	Page 2–6
12 Lessons	7–38
Tabernacle Passport and Fact Quiz	8
Original Skit	9–10
Tabernacle Times	33–34
Answers and Resources	39–40

Preview

God made a way of escape for his people and led them from slavery in Egypt into the wilderness of the Sinai where he fed them and gave them the Ten Commandments. Then he made a way for his people to worship him. He gave them specific directions for constructing the Tabernacle. Tabernacle is *Shakhan* in Hebrew and means "to dwell." The Tabernacle represented God's presence dwelling in the midst of his people.

God's plan for the Tabernacle was intentional. He designed every detail and he designed the path that the Priest was to take to illustrate how God desires his people to worship him.

The symbolism of the Tabernacle remains important for us today, pointing to God's plan for worship and salvation through Jesus Christ.

This workbook is designed to provide classes, small groups, and individuals with an opportunity to venture inside the Tabernacle as the High Priest would have thousands of years ago.

Take an opportunity to explore the significance of the materials used, consider the specific instructions for construction of the Tabernacle and the furnishings, and evaluate the impact on Christian worship.

✡ See the Tabernacle and furnishings as a picture of God's love and mercy and a preview of the coming Messiah.

✡ You may want to begin and end your study by taking the Tabernacle Fact Quiz on page 8.

✡ Consider setting up your meeting room to represent the size and furnishings of the Tabernacle. (Page 7)

✡ The pages with illustrations of the furnishings in the Tabernacle can be enlarged for use in setting up your room.

✡ Photocopy the worksheets and project sheets for individual or group use. You may want to enlarge or reduce some of the pages or use colored paper.

✡ Ideas for lessons and an outline for teachers can be found on page 3.

✡ A reproducible student worksheet to be used with many of the lessons is found on page 5.

✡ A reproducible pattern for making a passport for your Tabernacle journey is on page 8.

✡ Create your own class newspaper to tell about the Tabernacle and its time in Lesson 10. (Pages 33–34)

Pages 9–10 contain the script for "AMEN," a ten–minute drama, for use with your study of the Tabernacle. It could be used at the beginning to stimulate interest, or it could also be used at the end as a review for this important study of God's Word.

The Tabernacle Workbook
© 2004 RW Research, Inc.
Rose Publishing, LLC
P.O. Box 3473
Peabody, Massachusetts 01961-3473 USA
www.hendricksonrose.com

About the Author

Nancy Fisher loves to teach and see others get excited about the Bible. She has taught Sunday School, VBS, Day Camp, and Small Groups for 30+ years. She has written studies and devotions for family camps, youth camps and retreats. She enjoys theater and has written many short dramatic sketches as well as several full–length stage productions. She uses her gifts as an artist and writer to stimulate her teaching.

Through drama, discussion, object lessons, crafts, activities, special guests, service projects, small groups, field trips, and Bible study, she encourages students to know and trust God. She works to create an air of adventure and excitement in her classes.

Other Rose Publishing:

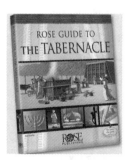

673X *Rose Guide to the Tabernacle* book

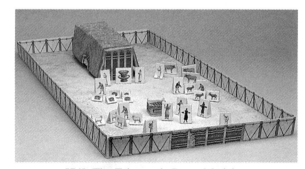

574L The Tabernacle Paper Model

LESSON 1: Introduction
Room set up, page 7
Rose wall chart *Tabernacle Cutaway* (551L)
Tabernacle Fact Quiz, page 8
Passport, page 8
"Amen" (skit) pages 9–10
Rose wall chart *The Tabernacle* (510L)

LESSON 2: The Outer Court
The Bronze Altar, page 11
The Bronze Laver, page 12
Rose wall chart *The Tabernacle* (510L)

LESSON 3: The Holy Place
The Golden Lampstand, page 13
The Table of Showbread, page 14
Rose wall chart *The Tabernacle* (510L)

LESSON 4: The Holy Place
The Altar of Incense, page 15
The Veil, page 16
Rose wall chart *The Tabernacle* (510L)

LESSON 5: The Holy of Holies
The Ark of the Covenant, page 17
The Ten Commandments, page 18
Rose wall chart *Ark of the Covenant* (546L)

LESSON 6: The Pattern of Worship
Details, pages 19–20
Worksheets, pages 21–22

LESSON 7: The High Priest
Description, page 23
Scripture Details, page 24
Jesus, Our High Priest, diagram, page 25
Symbols and Salvation, page 26

LESSON 8: Feasts, Fun, and Facts
Feasts and Holidays, page 27
God Made a Way, page 28
Fascinating Facts, page 29
My Calendar of Worship, page 30
Rose wall chart *Feasts of the Bible* (446L)

LESSON 9: You Are There
Tabernacle Visit, pages 31–32
Rose wall chart *Tabernacle Cutaway* (551L)

LESSON 10: Tabernacle Times
You're the Reporter, pages 33–34

LESSON 11: Tabernacle Details
Diagram, page 35
Map, page 36

LESSON 12: Review
God Made A Way, page 37
Path of Worship, page 38
Rose wall charts, *The Tabernacle* (510L),
Tabernacle Cutaway (551L), *Ark of the Covenant* (546L)
Rose wall chart *Feasts of the Bible* (446L)

WELCOME!

You are about to begin an incredible adventure as you discover God's plan for the Tabernacle and its meaning for us today.

TWELVE LESSONS

The Tabernacle Workbook and Guide can be used to prepare 12 or more different lessons. It can also be used to supplement lessons on various topics.

PHOTOCOPY PAGES FOR STUDENTS

Use the worksheets and Tabernacle diagrams to enrich each lesson.

USE WITH ROSE PUBLISHING WALL CHARTS

This workbook is designed as a companion to Rose wall charts *The Tabernacle* (510L), The *Tabernacle Cutaway* (551L), *Ark of the Covenant* (546L) and *Feasts of the Bible* (446L).

CREATE A TABERNACLE MODEL

Use the resources in this workbook to create a model of the Tabernacle in your classroom.

LEARN ABOUT TABERNACLE ITEMS

Each item in the Tabernacle had special significance. God gave specific directions for every design detail as well as all building materials.

LEARN ABOUT THE HIGH PRIEST

Every detail of the clothing and duties of the High Priest were part of God's plan for worship.

DISCOVER THE BIBLE HOLIDAYS

God designed annual celebrations to help his people remember his provision and protection.

USE AS RESOURCE MATERIAL

It can be used for individual or class lessons about the Tabernacle or to supplement purchased curriculum. You will also find this book an excellent resource for answering questions about the Tabernacle, the Ark of the Covenant, the High Priest, and more. Information on further resources and in–depth study of the Tabernacle for individuals or groups can be found on page 39.

TABERNACLE CROSSWORD

ACROSS

3. God showed Moses the pattern and furnishings for the _____. (Exodus 25:9)
6. Moses received the instruction for the Tabernacle on Mount _____. (Exodus 24:15-25:9)
7. The tribe of _____ had a total population of 53,400. (Numbers 1:20-42)
10. The priests carried the _____ ____ ____ _____ across the Jordan River when the Israelites entered the Promised Land. (Joshua 3:17)
12. The High Priest had two onyx _____, on which the names of the sons of Israel were engraved. (Exodus 28:9)
13. The tribe of _____ had a total population of 54,400. (Numbers 1:20-42)
15. The priests washed their hands and feet in the _____ Laver before going into the tent of meeting. (Exodus 30:18)
17. The curtain for the Holy of Holies was made out of blue, _____, and crimson yarn. (Exodus 36:35)
18. The _____ _____ was designed to hold seven lamps. (Exodus 25:31-37)
19. The tribe of _____ had a population of 62,700. (Numbers 1:20-42)

DOWN

1. The _____ ____ _____ was found in the holy place and was two cubits long and one cubit wide. (Exodus 25:23-30)
2. Aaron and his sons were the first _____ to serve in the Tabernacle. (Numbers 3:1-4)
3. The Ark of the Covenant contained the stone tablets with the _____ _____, Aaron's Rod, and a jar of manna. (Hebrews 9:4)
4. The Tabernacle was 100 _____ long. (Exodus 27:18)
5. Two _____ of gold were placed on each end of the mercy seat. (Exodus 25:18)
8. He was one of Aaron's sons who died because he offered unholy fire before the LORD. (Numbers 3:4)
9. The _____ _____ was five cubits long, five cubits wide, and three cubits high. (Exodus 27:1)
11. There are _____ loaves of bread placed on the Table of Showbread. (Leviticus 24:5)
14. The Altar of _____ was one cubit long, one cubit wide, and two cubits high. (Exodus 30:1-10)
16. The tribe of _____ had a population of 57,400. (Numbers 1:20-42)

It Happened in the Tabernacle	Old Testament Meaning	New Testament Meaning for Us Today
ENTER THE OUTER COURT (Exodus 27:9–19; 40:34–38) The only way through the 7.5' high fence into the Outer Court was through the one gate. The gate was covered by a beautiful high curtain of red, blue, and purple. Upon entering the Outer Court, the sight was one of fire, smoke, animals, people, and the Tabernacle. The Tabernacle was created of gold, silver, and tapestry with the cloud of God's Spirit resting upon it. See Exodus 26:15 for other materials.	■ God desired to dwell with his people. ■ The fence represented the barrier separating God's people from the world. ■ God could only be approached in the way he designed, through repentance and sacrifice.	God is with us: Jesus is God in the flesh dwelling among His people: Matthew 1:22–23; John 1:14; 14:8–10 God is majestic and holy: Psalm 29; 104; Isaiah 66:1 Sin and repentance are serious: Psalm 15:1–2; Luke 18:9–14; Romans 1:18–20; 3:23
BRONZE ALTAR SACRIFICE (Exodus 27:1–8; Leviticus 1:1–4) After a sacrifice was approved, it was laid on the 7.5' x 7.5' x 4.5' altar. The priest's hands were placed on the animal's head as it was sacrificed to represent repentance and the blood of the animal as payment for sin.	■ An acceptable sacrifice was perfect and valuable, not flawed or sickly. ■ Sin was serious. Only blood, which meant life, could pay for sin. ■ Laying hands on its head meant you identified with the sacrificed animal.	There is a penalty for sin: Rom. 6:23; Heb. 9:22 Jesus was perfect and the final sacrifice for all time. His sacrifice was necessary and complete: Exodus 30:10; Isaiah 53:4–7; John 1:29; Romans 3:21–25; 5:8–10; Hebrews 9:13–14; 1 Peter 1:18–19; Revelation 5:6–13
THE PRIEST (Exodus 28:1–5, 40; Leviticus 1:5–9) The priest was from the line of Levi, the tribe of Aaron. He was dressed in colorful garments which were designed by God and matched the tapestries. Part of his responsibility was to catch the blood from the sacrifices and sprinkle some of it around the altar. The smoke from the burning sacrifice rose to God for acceptance. Most Israelites could go no further, and when finished they would leave the courtyard.	■ Individual Israelites could not approach God directly, only through the priests, God's chosen mediators. ■ Animals' blood paid the penalty of sin. ■ Sincere repentance and sacrifice were pleasing to God.	Jesus Christ is our mediator: 1 Timothy 2:5; Hebrews 12:22–24 Christ's blood was the final, perfect sacrifice and covers our sin: John 3:16; Romans 5:8–9; Ephesians 1:7; Colossians 1:19–22; 1 Peter 1:1–2 Christ's sacrifice is pleasing to God: Psalm 51:16; Ephesians 5:2
THE BRONZE BASIN (Exodus 30:17–21; 38:8) Also known as the laver, it was located between the altar and the Tabernacle. It was a shallow basin of water that gleamed like mirrors. The priests bathed their hands and feet before entering the Tabernacle.	■ Hand and foot washing represented sanctification, becoming pure and holy. ■ Serving God required cleansing from sin and striving for holiness.	We have a priestly service: 1 Peter 2:5; Rev. 1:4–6 We are called to be holy: John 13:6–9; James 4:7–8 We are washed through God's Word: John 15:3; 17:7; Ephesians 5:26
THE HOLY PLACE (Exodus 25:23–26, 25:37; 30:1–10) The priests opened the curtain to enter the 15' x 30' Holy Place, the first section of the Tabernacle. Their duties included keeping the seven lamps on the Golden Lampstand burning constantly, tending the 12 loaves of bread displayed on the Gold Table, and offering prayers for the people at the Golden Altar of Incense which stood before the curtain leading to the second section of the Tabernacle, the Holy of Holies.	■ Light represented God's presence. ■ Bread stood for thankfulness for God's provision and the joy of fellowship at the table with him. ■ Incense represented constant prayer.	Jesus Christ is the Light of the World: John 1:1–9; Revelation 21:22–23 All believers are the light of the world: Matthew 5:14–16; Philippians 2:14–15; Revelation 1:10–19 Jesus Christ is the Bread of Life: Lk. 22:19; Jn. 6:35 We are to always give thanks: 1 Corinthians 16:21; 1 Thessalonians 5:18
THE HIGH PRIEST (Exodus 28; Leviticus 16) The High Priest could enter the Holy of Holies. This occurred one day each year on Yom Kippur, the Day of Atonement. After sacrificing outside, he removed his outer garments with the gemstones representing the 12 tribes. He brought incense and blood to sprinkle on the Ark of the Covenant on behalf of the people. After exiting, the High Priest sent the scapegoat into the desert, bearing the sins of the people away.	■ Only one mediator, the High Priest, went before God to plead for the entire nation. ■ Even with all the other sacrifices, still more was needed to atone for the all-pervasive sin. ■ Guilt could be atoned for and sent away.	Jesus is our High Priest: Romans 3:21–26; 5:8–10; Heb. 4:14–16; 9:11–15, 24–28; 10:1–14; 13:11–13 Jesus intercedes for us: Romans 8:34; Heb. 7:23–25 The power of sin is banished: Psalm 103:8–12; Romans 7:14–25; Hebrews 13:11–12
THE HOLY OF HOLIES (Exodus 25:10–22; 26:31–34; Hebrews 9:4) Only the High Priest could open the 15-foot–high veil embroidered with guardian cherubim and enter the presence of God. The 15' x 15' Holy of Holies held the gold-covered Ark of the Covenant. The Ark contained the tablets of the Law, Aaron's rod, and a pot of manna. The gold cover, God's throne or the Mercy Seat, had two cherubim on top. The cherubim faced down, wings pointing toward the place of God's presence.	■ Sin separates us from God. ■ God was not represented by a statue; God is Spirit. ■ Contents of the Ark illustrated God's desire to teach, provide and dwell with us. ■ God offered mercy so his sinful people could approach him.	Veil of the Holy of Holies: Genesis 3:24; Matthew 27:50–51; Hebrews 10:19–20 God is Spirit: Isaiah 66:1; John 4:24 God teaches and provides: John 1:17; Acts 17:24–27; Galatians 3:24–25 The throne of God and the Mercy Seat: Psalm 80:1; Hebrews 4:16; 1 Peter 1:10–12

The Tabernacle

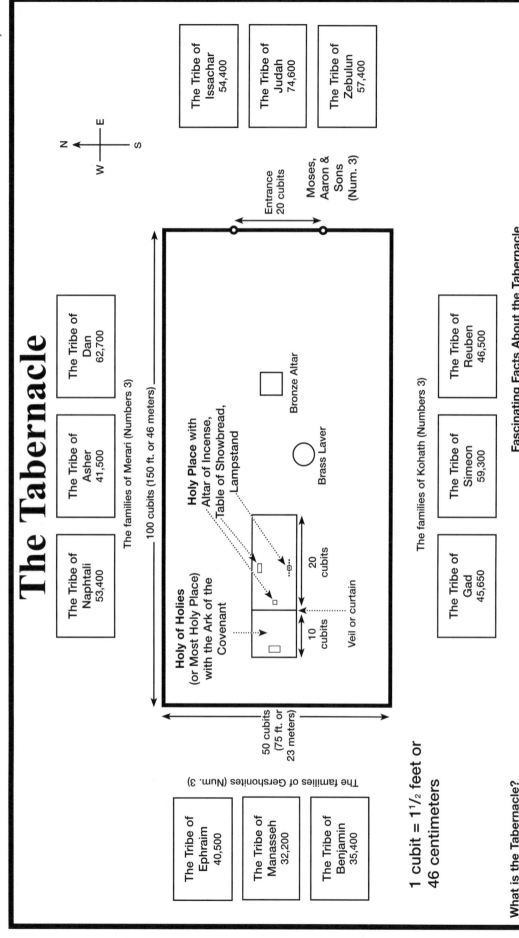

The Tribe of Naphtali 53,400

The Tribe of Asher 41,500

The Tribe of Dan 62,700

The families of Merari (Numbers 3)

The Tribe of Ephraim 40,500

The Tribe of Manasseh 32,200

The Tribe of Benjamin 35,400

The families of Gershonites (Num. 3)

The Tribe of Issachar 54,400

The Tribe of Judah 74,600

The Tribe of Zebulun 57,400

N E W S

Entrance 20 cubits

Moses, Aaron & Sons (Num. 3)

Holy of Holies (or Most Holy Place) with the Ark of the Covenant

Holy Place with Altar of Incense, Table of Showbread, Lampstand

Bronze Altar

Brass Laver

100 cubits (150 ft. or 46 meters)

50 cubits (75 ft. or 23 meters)

20 cubits

10 cubits

Veil or curtain

The families of Kohath (Numbers 3)

The Tribe of Gad 45,650

The Tribe of Simeon 59,300

The Tribe of Reuben 46,500

1 cubit = 1½ feet or 46 centimeters

What is the Tabernacle?

The Tabernacle was a moveable "tent of meeting" that God commanded Moses to build. (Read Exodus 25:1-2 and 25:8-9.) God wanted to dwell among his people, the Israelites. He wanted to have fellowship with them and be able to communicate with them (Ex. 25:22).

The Tabernacle and its courtyard were constructed according to a pattern set by God, not by Moses. We study the Tabernacle to understand the steps that the Lord laid out for a sinful people to approach a holy God. The Tabernacle became the place that God dwelt with his people for 400 years: from the Exodus until the time of King Solomon, when the Temple was built.

The Tabernacle was in the center of the Israelite camp. The 12 Tribes of Israel were encamped around it. The figures in the boxes refer to the number of males age 20 or over in each tribe. The total would be 603,550.

Fascinating Facts About the Tabernacle

- There are 50 chapters in the Bible that discuss the Tabernacle.
- The Tabernacle would have fit in half of a football or soccer field.
- The Tabernacle of the Old Testament was a "shadow" of things in heaven. Hebrews 8:1-5 tells us that the real Tabernacle is in heaven. This is where Jesus Himself is our high priest (Heb. 8:2).
- The Tabernacle was built using many expensive materials: gold, silver, bronze, precious woods, and rare cloth. In modern terms the cost would exceed $1 million. Offerings from the Israelites paid for the materials. (Ex. 35:22-36:3)
- The Israelites were so generous they gave more than was needed. Moses had to command them to stop giving. (Ex. 36:6)

JOURNEY THROUGH THE TABERNACLE

■ **Room Setup.** Whether you are using a regular classroom, large meeting room, or a private living room, it is exciting and meaningful to set up your meeting space to reflect the Tabernacle, or some part of it. Remember that the Tabernacle was twice as long as it was wide. The entry gate was 30 feet wide! The Holy of Holies was only 15 feet square. Set up whatever space you have for your study of the Tabernacle.

■ **How big was the Tabernacle?** Display a Tabernacle wall chart such as *Tabernacle Cutaway* (551L). Considering that the dimensions of the Tabernacle were 150 feet by 75 feet, a 10:1 ratio would be 15 feet by 7.5 feet. If your room will accommodate that size, it will give you some idea of the area of the Tabernacle. If not, modify it as necessary.

■ **Parking Lot Measurements.** Try marking out the actual measurements on a large parking lot or playground so you can get a feel for how big it was.

■ **Furnishings of the Tabernacle.** If you have access to tables, basins, or candelabra, they could represent the altar, laver, lampstand, or other items. Use them to furnish your room. You may want to visit a local thrift store or neighborhood garage sale for three–dimensional items or just use cardboard boxes and tape photocopied illustrations on them. You could also make cutouts of the furniture and spray them with gold paint. The following lessons include illustrations of the items of furniture listed in the Bible for the Tabernacle. Photocopy and color the drawings or photocopy them on gold-colored paper to represent the bronze and gold of the original items.

■ **Walls of the Tabernacle.** You could hang sheets on the walls to represent the animal skins and cloth walls of the Tabernacle.

■ **God's Design for Worship.** The location and placement of everything in the Tabernacle had special significance for the people of Israel as well as for the priests. By following that plan and pattern, your class will be able to better relate to God's purpose in designing the Tabernacle for worship. Your journey through the Tabernacle may even help you design your own personal plan for worship.

TABERNACLE FACT QUIZ

See page 8

The quiz (above the dotted line on page 8) is designed to reveal students' knowledge about the Tabernacle before using this workbook and after. Make two photocopies for each person in the class. At the first session, ask students to indicate their name and date and then answer the questions. Repeat these instructions at your final meeting. When class members have finished answering the questions the second time, have them compare their answers with the first quiz. This will offer the class a good opportunity for review, questions, and comments.

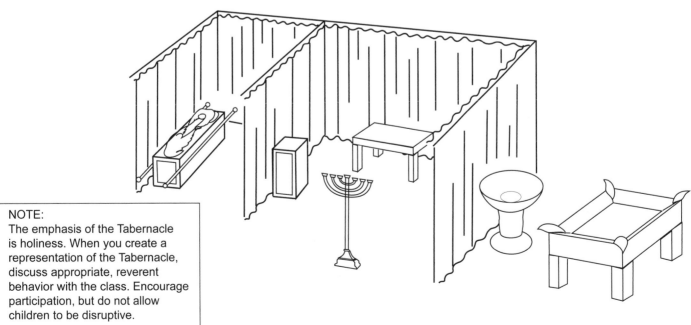

NOTE:
The emphasis of the Tabernacle is holiness. When you create a representation of the Tabernacle, discuss appropriate, reverent behavior with the class. Encourage participation, but do not allow children to be disruptive.

TABERNACLE FACT QUIZ

NAME _____   DATE _____

1____ The Tabernacle was designed by:
a. Moses   b. Aaron   c. God

2____ "Tabernacle" means:
a. temple   b. dwelling   c. library

3____ The Tabernacle was set up at the edge of camp.   T or F

4____ The Tabernacle represented God's Spirit with his people. T or F

5____ The Tabernacle was built to house: a. a stone altar
b. the Ark of the Covenant   c. treasure from Egypt

6____ The outer wall was covered with porpoise skin.   T or F

7____ Width of the front gate was: a. 30 feet b. 40 feet c. 60 feet

8____ The Tabernacle had how many sections?   a. 5 b. 12 c. 3

9____ The Holy of Holies was a special room designed for
the Ark of the Covenant.   T or F

10____ During what holiday did the High Priest enter the Holy of
Holies? a. Passover b. Feast of Tabernacles c. Yom Kippur

11____ The bronze laver was used by the people to wash
before prayer.   T or F

12____ The altar of sacrifices was used for animals and grain. T or F

13____ The table of showbread held how many loaves of bread?
a. 12 b. 16 c. 20

14____ Only incense from a special recipe was to be burnt in the
Tabernacle. T or F

15____ The gold in the lampstand weighed:
a. 100 lbs.   b. 125 lbs.   c. 200 lbs.

16. Circle the items that were in the outer court of the Tabernacle:
golden lampstand water jars altar of sacrifice bronze laver
Ark of the Covenant table of showbread animal cages cherubim
offering chest altar of incense acacia wood chairs priestly robes

17. Circle the items that were in the Holy Place of the Tabernacle:
golden lampstand water jars altar of sacrifice bronze laver
Ark of the Covenant table of showbread animal cages cherubim
offering chest altar of incense acacia wood chairs priestly robes

18. Circle the items that were in the Ark of the Covenant:
Ten Commandments gold coins jar of manna lamb bone
matzo Aaron's rod 3 stones from Mt. Sinai Moses' sandal

....

Student Passports Use the lower part of this page to make student passports. Photocopy and cut along the solid line, fold back along the dotted line and glue. Then fold in half. Let students use their passports to mark their journey through the Tabernacle. Have them color one jewel on the breastplate at the completion of each lesson.

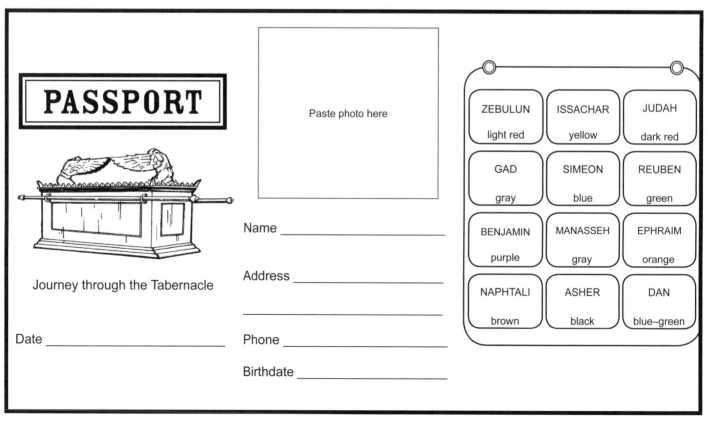

AMEN

PLOT: Three Sunday school students (adult or teen) find themselves without a teacher/leader and responsible for the next class.

CAST: Kelly, K.C., Kamden   PROPS: Notes, Bible

ACTION: Drama opens with Kelly, K.C. and Kamden looking bewildered while holding notes they have just opened.

K. C.: He can't be serious. Mr. Martin wants us to lead the class while he's out of town. I don't think so!

KAM: Don't you have to have a special degree or something to be the leader?

K.C.: Hey, I'm happy just being a follower.

KELLY: Come on, you two, how hard could it be?

KAM: Easy for you to say.

KELLY: Hey. You lead a song, say a prayer, read the Bible, and . . . .

K.C.: Say "AMEN!" a lot.

KAM: You think that will fill up an hour?

K.C.: Our class is only an hour?

KELLY: I vote for getting serious. We're responsible for leading people in worship. You can joke about it all you want, but I'm pretty sure that God takes it seriously.

KAM.: OK, OK. Anyone got a copy of last week's outline?

K. C.: Sure. All we need to do is change the songs, update the prayer list, and . . .

KELLY: Hold it! That's your definition of "serious"?

KAM: Well . . .

K.C.: Is this going to take much longer?

KAM: Do you realize that people will be watching us?

KELLY: Do you realize that God will be watching us?

K.C.: Remember me? I'm the follower. So, where's that outline?

KAM: We're sunk!

K.C.: It's hopeless.

KELLY: It is not hopeless.

KAM: You have an idea?

K.C.: An idea would be good.

KELLY: Well, I was just thinking about last week's lesson.

KAM: Great!

K.C.: Why didn't I think of that?

KELLY: Hey, look! I found the outline. (Kam scans it.) Look...a...here....

K.C.: Let me see that. (K. C. looks over shoulder.) Here it is . . .
the T–A–B (K. C. begins to spell it.)

KELLY: The Tabernacle!

K.C.: R–i–g–h–t!

KAM: We're sunk.

K.C.: It's hopeless.

KELLY: You two are hopeless. Remember what Pastor Martin said?

KAM: Of course!

K.C.: AMEN!

KELLY: A . . . A . . . A. He said even though the Tabernacle was a real, physical structure once, it was and still is a pattern for worship.

K.C.: How do you remember all that?

KAM: Do you think we can do that?

K. C.: Do what? All I remember are sacrifices and stuff . . .

KELLY: I said "pattern."

KAM: Yeah, a pattern is good. But it's not on this outline.

K. C.: So where's the pattern?

KELLY: (holds up a Bible)

K. C.: Oh, that pattern.

KAM: I remember! I remember! It's in Exodus.

KELLY: Amazingly, you are right!

K. C.: Go, Kamden!

KAM: (Looking at the outline) Here it is! Beginning in Exodus 25.

K. C.: I'm getting a good feeling about this.

KELLY: I think we should begin at the gate.

K. C.: The gate, as in one?

KELLY: Yes, there was only one gate.

KAM: Like Jesus! He's the only way to God!

KELLY: Exactly.

K. C.: AMEN!

KAM: But we have to confess our sin . . .

K. C.: And say we're sorry.

KELLY: Yes! You've got it! So confession and repentance brings us to the Altar of Sacrifice.

K. C.: I knew there was sacrifice.

KELLY: There has to be a way to pay for our sin. In the Bible, animals were sacrificed to pay for the sins of the people.

K. C.: But Jesus was the sacrifice for our sin.

KELLY: Exactly! He was the final blood sacrifice.

KAM: OK. What's next?

KELLY: The bronze laver.

K. C.: What's a laver?

KELLY: It was a basin where the priests washed.

KAM: Just like Jesus washed our sins away.

K. C.: AMEN!

KELLY: You're great! Let's keep going.

KAM: I'm beginning to like this.

KELLY: Now we have to enter the Holy Place.

K. C.: Where were we before?

KELLY: The altar and the laver were in the courtyard. Everyone could go there. Only the priest . . . .

KAM: . . . could go inside the Holy Place.

The Tabernacle Workbook

KELLY: Exactly. The first thing inside the Holy Place was the golden lampstand with seven branches.

KAM: I get it, I get it! Lampstand, light . . . Jesus said he was the light of the world.

K. C.: And I know that song from Psalm 119: "Thy Word is a lamp unto my feet and a light unto my path."

KELLY: And in another verse the Bible tells us that WE are children of light which means . . .

KAM: . . . that we need to tell everyone about Jesus' sacrifice and washing away our sin!

K. C.: AMEN!

(All give each other a high five.)

KAM: Keep going, Kelly.

KELLY: OK. Across from the lampstand was the table of showbread.

K.C.: Like, show me the bread?

KELLY: It was just bread, OK. There was a special table in the Holy Place and there was always bread on it. Twelve loaves for the . . .

KAM: . . . twelve tribes!

K. C.: And, Jesus said he was the bread of life.

KELLY: The Bible is full of verses about bread. I think the point is that God will take care of our physical needs.

K. C.: Wait a minute. I'm remembering a verse. The Bible says that man shall not live by bread alone but by every word from the mouth of God.

KELLY: You are so right! God will provide for our physical AND spiritual life.

K. C.: AMEN!

KAM: This is so good. What else is in the Holy Place?

(Kamden looks in the Bible and Kelly points to the place.)

KAM: Oh, oh. Another altar.

K. C.: But . . .

KELLY: The altar in the Holy Place is smaller. It's called the altar of incense.

K. C.: So, they probably burned incense on it . . .

K. C.: And it smelled good.

KELLY: Just like our prayers and praises smell sweet to God.

KAM: So, we make God happy with our prayers and praises?

K. C.: Are we good, or what?

KELLY: God is good, K.C.

K. C.: AMEN. That's what I meant . . .

KAM: We know.

KELLY: Hey, we're almost done.

KAM: Oh, no.

KELLY: Think about it . . . what's left?

KAM: a . . . a . . . a

K. C.: a . . . a . . . a

KELLY: OK Let's review.

KAM: Jesus is our gate to God. And, he's the sacrifice that washes away our sin.

K. C.: He's the light revealing God's love and goodness and we're the light, telling the world about Jesus Christ and God's plan.

KAM: Jesus is the Bread of Life.

K. C.: And so is God's Word.

KELLY: And our praise is like sweet incense to God.

K. C.: Sounds like we just about covered it all!

KAM: What IS left?

KELLY: There's one more section to the Tabernacle. The Holy of Holies and the Ark . . . .

K. C.: The Ark of the Covenant!

KELLY: Yes, the Ark of the Covenant, and that's a whole lesson all by itself.

K. C.: In ten words or less.

KAM: Didn't Pastor Martin say that people died when they touched it because it was so holy to God?

K. C.: It had gold angels on top.

KELLY: And . . .

KAM: And . . .

KELLY: And the Mercy Seat.

KAM: I get it! God's mercy!

K. C.: It's all about God's mercy!

KAM: I'm remembering another memory verse, "If we confess our sins, he is faithful and just and will forgive us our sins and purify us from all unrighteousness."

K. C.: Oh, yeah, that's mercy all right.

KELLY: Well, we're done.

K. C.: AMEN!

KELLY: Almost, . . . how does this affect worship?

KAM: That's easy. We enter church through the door, which reminds us of Jesus being the gate, the only way to God.

K. C.: We see the altar up front and that reminds us that Jesus was the sacrifice to save us and wash us from our sin.

KAM: When we see the candles in the church, that reminds us that Jesus is the Light of the World and that we are Children of the Light. The whole world needs to know about Jesus.

K. C.: And, there's a Bible on the altar and sometimes there's bread on it, too, so we can thank Jesus for being the Bread of Life for our bodies and our spirits.

KAM: When we sing and pray, we're offering God a sweet fragrance.

KELLY: And the pastor reminds us that God accepts Jesus as our sacrifice, forgives us, and gives us mercy.

KAM: Kelly, this was great! I'll never look at worship the same way again.

K. C.: AMEN!

KAM: But we still have a problem.

KELLY: Huh?

KAM: Do you think one hour will be enough?

KELLY, K. C. & KAMDEN: AMEN!

SCRIPTURE

Exodus 27:1–8;
Leviticus 4:7,
10, 18

HEBREW

The word *altar* is
from the Hebrew
mizbech (miz–bake)
which means
"slaughter place."

JOURNEY INFORMATION

Upon entering the gate, one
would arrive in the outer
court. The bronze altar and
the bronze laver were the only
items there. The outer court
was the place for atonement,
worship, and cleansing in
preparation to meet God. One
could not enter the Holy Place
without coming by way of the
gate, the altar, and the laver.

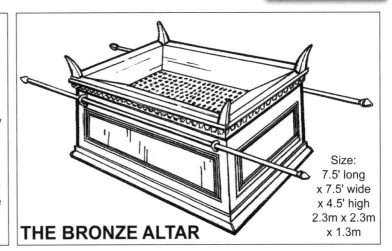

THE BRONZE ALTAR

Size:
7.5' long
x 7.5' wide
x 4.5' high
2.3m x 2.3m
x 1.3m

THE GATE

Two of the Psalms give a
clear picture of the proper
attitude in relation to God's
house.
■ **Psalm 122:1** I rejoiced with
those who said "let us go to
the house of the LORD."
■ **Psalm 100:4** Enter his
gates with thanksgiving and
His courts with praise.

Share with a friend what
excites you about going to
church.

THE ALTAR

Altars in the Old Testament
were significant to God's
people as places to offer
sacrifice, and more importantly,
as places to meet God and
remember his covenant. Why
did these men build altars?
■ **Noah** (Genesis 8:18–20)
■ **Abraham** (Genesis 22:9–14)
■ **Moses (**Exodus 24:3–4)
■ **Joshua** (Joshua 8:30–31)

LOCATION

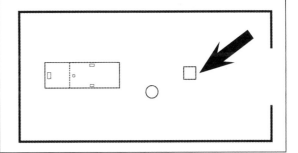

ITEM INFORMATION
The Bronze Altar

Made of acacia wood, the Bronze Altar was square with
horns and rings at each corner. It was 7.5 square feet by
4.5 feet high. The wood was covered with bronze and it was
carried by bronze plated poles. Bronze utensils were used
on the Bronze Altar.

The most–used piece of furniture in the Tabernacle was the
Bronze Altar, also known as the Altar of Burnt Offering. It was
used all day as people came to offer sacrifices.
The two types of sacrifices offered on the Bronze Altar were
the sin–guilt sacrifices and the gift–peace offerings. Sacrifice
is necessary to relate to God. (Leviticus 17:11; 1 Corinthians
2:2; Hebrews 9:22) Blood sacrifices were offered for sin
and guilt to make atonement and to reconcile with God.
Gift offerings included grain offerings, peace offerings, and
burnt offerings. They were sacrificed for consecration and
dedication to God.

ACTIVITY
Questions for Discussion

Pick a question and answer it on another sheet of
paper.

● Consider that the Bronze Altar's name
meant "slaughter place," and that it would
be used to burn sacrifices. Why do you think
God gave such specific directions for the
design and construction of the altar?

● Think about how seriously God takes sin as
reflected in the Old
Testament system
of sacrifice. Read
Colossians 2:13–14
and tell what it
means to have your
sins forgiven (nailed
to the cross).

ACTIVITY

Read Luke 6:37–38; Acts
13:38; Ephesians 1:7–8;
4:32; and James 5:16.
Find a current newspaper
article that shows how our
culture reacts to sin today.

The Outer Court

SCRIPTURE

Exodus 30:17–21

HEBREW

A laver is a basin for ceremonial cleansing. The Hebrew word *kiyor* means "laver."

LATIN

The word *laver* comes from the Latin word *lavatorium*. The Spanish word *lavar* (to wash) and the English word *lavatory* also come from the same word.

WORD STUDY
CLEAN

Look up the word "clean" and related words in a concordance and explore some of the Bible references.

ITEM INFORMATION
The Bronze Laver

The laver was a large basin for ceremonial washing. The size is not given in the Bible, but it is described as made of bronze and mounted on a base. Priests needed to cleanse themselves before meeting with God.

FACT

Exodus 38:8 says that the laver was made from mirrors. The Israelites brought polished copper mirrors with them from Egypt.

JOURNEY INFORMATION
SANCTIFICATION

The bronze laver represents the ministry of sanctification.

■ Sanctification is an ongoing process. It is the process of being cleansed from sin once, and then continually being cleansed from sin.

■ Priests bathed their entire body at the laver when they were ordained. (Exodus 29:4) Following ordination, priests just washed their hands and feet every time they approached God to maintain their cleanliness.

■ What does Psalm 24:3–6 associate with clean hands?

■ The laver is a picture of believers in Christ being saved once, and maintaining that cleanliness before God by continual confession and acknowledgment of sin. (John 13:3–10; Titus 3:5)

THE BRONZE LAVER

Size: None indicated

LOCATION

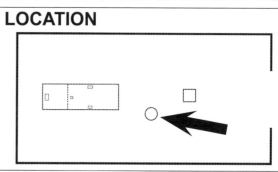

ACTIVITY
The Theme of Water and Sanctification

Water is a continual theme in the Bible. It sustains all life and it is necessary for cleanliness. Pick one passage: Genesis 6–9; 2 Kings 5:1–14; Jonah 1–2; Matthew 27:24; John 2:1–11; John 5:1–9; John 7:37–38; John 13:2–10.

Write about a Bible event where water is important. _____

_____

Tell one thing that happened. _____

_____

How would the situation have been different without water? _____

_____

Compare this Bible event to information on sanctification. _____

_____

_____

The Holy Place

SCRIPTURE

Exodus 25:31–40; 27:20–21; 37:17–24

FACT

In Bible times, lamps were saucers of clay or metal. One edge was a bowl to hold oil and the other edge was pinched in to hold a wick.

By the first century many clay lamps had become beautiful works of art.

WEIGHT IN GOLD

The golden lampstand weighed 75 pounds. What would its value be using today's price for gold?

$_____

(Look up the price of gold in the newspaper or on the Internet.)

JOURNEY INFORMATION
The Holy Place

The Holy Place is also known as the sanctuary. The inner curtains included one of goats' hair, which represented sacrificial offerings, plus curtains of white, blue, purple, and scarlet linen. These are the colors often attributed to God.

The outer curtains around the Tabernacle were created from rams' skins and dyed red to represent the blood sacrifices that covers our sin.

The outermost covering was made of porpoises' skins, which are extremely durable.

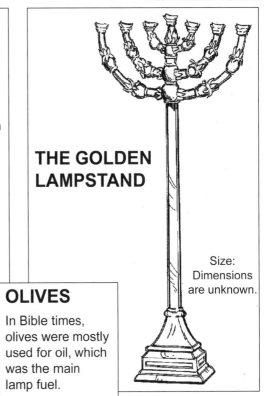

THE GOLDEN LAMPSTAND

Size: Dimensions are unknown.

OLIVES

In Bible times, olives were mostly used for oil, which was the main lamp fuel.

ITEM INFORMATION   The Golden Lampstand

- Although sometimes referred to as the golden candlesticks, that term can be misleading. The lampstand was actually seven oil lamps connected together. (Candles weren't developed until Roman times.)
- The Golden Lampstand was constructed according to a pattern shown to Moses.
- It was to be made of one talent (75 pounds) of pure gold.
- The lampstand was designed to provide light for the Tabernacle. The lampstand was the first item seen upon entering the Tabernacle as a reminder to His people that God is light.
- A priest's duty was to trim the wicks and keep the lamps lit. (Leviticus 24:1–4) The lesson for believers is to pay attention to the light of Christ living within us; it is God's witness to the world.
- There are several references to light in the New Testament. (John 8:12; John 9:5; Ephesians 5:8; Philippians 2:15; James 1:17)

LOCATION

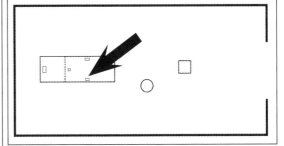

ACTIVITY
Make a simple clay lamp

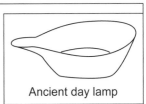

Ancient day lamp

In Bible times, people lit a small wick in some olive oil in a lamp like this illustration to produce light.

To make a small lamp, begin with a lump of wet clay and flatten it into the shape of a pancake.

Next, shape up the sides to make a shallow bowl, then pinch in one side to resemble the illustration above.

HEBREW

The Hebrew word *chanukah* is pronounced ha–noo–ka with a very harsh "h" at the beginning of the word. It means "dedication."

THE HOLIDAY OF CHANUKAH

The Feast of Dedication is also known as Chanukah or the Festival of Lights. It has been celebrated by Jewish people since 156 BC when the lamp giving light to the Temple was relit and burned miraculously for eight days.

Jesus celebrated Chanukah when he was in Jerusalem. (John 10:22–23)

The Holy Place

SCRIPTURE

Exodus
25:23–30;
37:10–16;
Leviticus
24:59

HEBREW

In Hebrew,
Bethlehem
means "house
of bread."

NEW TESTAMENT REFERENCES

Matthew 4:4
John 6:35, 51

JOURNEY INFORMATION
The Table of Showbread

The Table of Showbread was also called the "Table of the Bread of the Presence."

Bread (food) is necessary for physical health. Spiritually, we also need our "daily bread" from God.

ITEM INFORMATION
The Table of Showbread

■ The table was a wooden rectangle overlaid with gold. It had rings at the corners to insert poles for carrying.

■ Golden utensils were used for serving at the Table of Showbread.

■ Bread was always to be on the table, which is an illustration that God is always waiting for fellowship with us.

■ Twelve loaves were to be made from fine flour and placed on the table before God. The priests ate the bread.

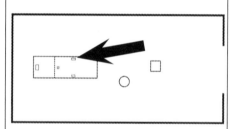

Size:
3' long x 1.5' wide x 2.25' high
92cm x 41cm x 69cm

THE TABLE OF SHOWBREAD

LOCATION

ACTIVITY
The Provision of God

Consider these four Bible passages and write why bread is significant in each.

Deuteronomy 8:3 _____

_____

1 Kings 17:8–16 _____

_____

Matthew 6:11 _____

_____

Luke 9:10–17 _____

_____

ACTIVITY

Matzah is the unleavened bread God commanded his people to bake and eat at the first Passover. Jews have been eating matzah for over 3,000 years. Have your class experiment with making some unleavened bread. Put 2 cups of flour in a bowl and slowly mix in enough water to make a soft dough. Sprinkle flour on a working surface and roll out or pat your dough into thin, flat bread. Pierce bread with a fork several times to discourage rising, and bake at 350°F until light brown.

Matzah is dry, so you may want to serve it with butter, jelly or other topping.

The Holy Place

SCRIPTURE

Exodus 30:1–10, 34–38; 37:25–29; Leviticus 10:1–3

SPECIAL RECIPE

Exodus 30:34–38

God gave Moses a specific recipe for the incense to be burned on the Altar of Incense.

FACT

The Magi brought incense to Jesus.

(Matthew 2:10–11)

ITEM INFORMATION
The Altar of Incense

■ The altar was square, made of wood, and overlaid with gold. It had rings in the corners for carrying poles.

■ The fire for the incense came from the Bronze Altar in the outer court.

■ The Altar of Incense sat in front of the veil concealing the Holy of Holies.

JOURNEY INFORMATION
The Altar of Incense

■ The final stop in the Holy Place was the Altar of Incense.

■ With the assurance that God is the Light and Bread of Life, the priest approached the Altar of Incense two times each day.

■ Incense rising with smoke is a picture of our prayers rising to heaven. (Psalm 141:1–2)

■ Preparation for prayer requires repentance and a clean heart. (Psalm 50:23, Proverbs 15:8)

NEW TESTAMENT REFERENCES

■ At the time of the incense offering, it was the custom to gather for prayer. (Luke 1:10)

■ Zechariah was burning incense in the Temple when the angel Gabriel visited him with the news that his wife, Elizabeth, would have a son. (Luke 1:8–25)

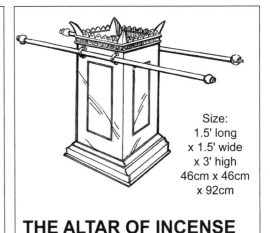

Size: 1.5' long x 1.5' wide x 3' high 46cm x 46cm x 92cm

THE ALTAR OF INCENSE

LOCATION

ACTIVITY

Read Psalm 147:1–9. Write a prayer praising and thanking God:

_____

_____

_____

_____

_____

_____

_____

_____

ACTIVITY

CINNAMON CLAY ORNAMENT

Mix together 1/2 cup of ground cinnamon and 4 ounces of applesauce. Knead with hands until mixture is smooth and "clay–like." Roll or pat mixture to about 1/2 inch thick. Use dry cinnamon on hands and utensils to prevent sticking.

Cut into shapes (cross, star, heart, etc.) that remind you to pray and praise God. Use a cookie cutter or plastic knife to cut your shapes; then punch a small hole with a straw.

Air–dry for one week, turning once a day for even drying. When firm and dry, thread a piece of ribbon through the hole. Hang your ornament in a special place so you can enjoy the sweet fragrance and remember that your prayers are a sweet fragrance to God.

SCRIPTURE

Exodus 26:31–35; 36:35–38

ITEM INFORMATION
The Veil

■ Instructions for creating the Veil: Exodus 26:31–34; 36:35–36

■ According to Jewish tradition, there were two veils in Herod's temple. Both were 60 feet long, 30 feet wide and 4 inches thick. They were made of 72 squares sewn together. They were so heavy it took 300 priests to hang them.

■ God gave Ezekiel a vision of the Holy Temple and the Holy of Holies. (Ezekiel 41)

JOURNEY INFORMATION
The Veil and the Holy Place

■ The Veil separated the Holy Place from the Holy of Holies.

■ The Ark of the Covenant and the Mercy Seat were secure inside the Holy of Holies.

■ The High Priest was permitted to open the Veil and enter the Holy of Holies once a year on Yom Kippur to ask forgiveness from God. When sprinkled with atoning blood, the Mercy Seat was changed from the judgment place into the Throne of Grace.

■ The Ark of the Covenant is not mentioned after Jerusalem was invaded by Babylon in 586 BC.

FACT

Simultaneously with the death of Jesus Christ, the Veil was ripped from top to bottom. His sacrifice changed the veil from a barrier to an open door. It can be said that Jesus' atonement invited sinful people to enter the presence of God. (Matthew 27:51)

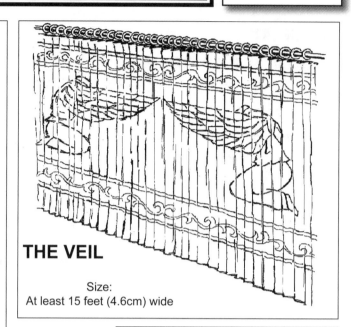

THE VEIL

Size:
At least 15 feet (4.6cm) wide

LOCATION

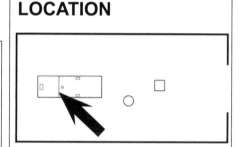

OLD TESTAMENT ACTIVITY (Read the verses and write the answers.)

Exodus 26:31–34: What colors of yarn were used to make the Veil? _____

.. What were the hanging hooks made of? _____

.. What two places in the Tabernacle did the Veil separate? _____

1 Kings 8:1–5: Who ordered the Ark of the Covenant brought to the Temple in Jerusalem? _____

2 Chronicles 3:1–17: On what mountain did Solomon build the Temple in Jerusalem? _____

Ezekiel 10:18; 11:23: In Ezekiel's vision and prophecy, what departed from the temple? _____

NEW TESTAMENT ACTIVITY (Read the verses and fill in the blanks.)

Heb. 9:11–12: Jesus Christ is our _____

Heb. 10:10: We have been made _____ by Jesus' sacrifice.

Heb. 10:19–22: The blood of Jesus gives believers the confidence to _____

The Holy of Holies

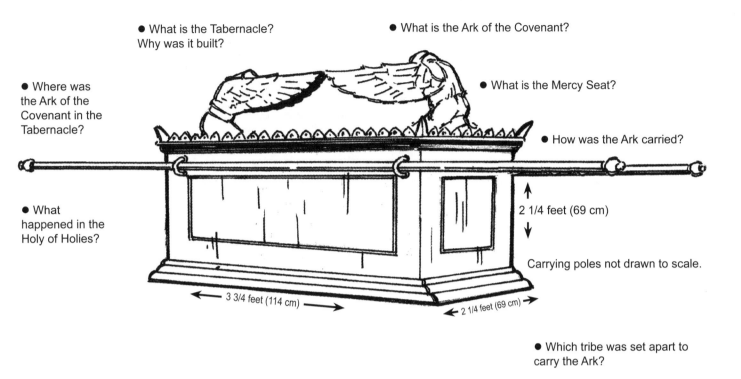

- What is the Tabernacle? Why was it built?
- What is the Ark of the Covenant?
- Where was the Ark of the Covenant in the Tabernacle?
- What is the Mercy Seat?
- How was the Ark carried?
- What happened in the Holy of Holies?

2 1/4 feet (69 cm)

Carrying poles not drawn to scale.

← 3 3/4 feet (114 cm) →

← 2 1/4 feet (69 cm) →

- Which tribe was set apart to carry the Ark?

The Ark of the Covenant was the place where God said he would meet with and talk to Moses. (Exodus 25:22)

The Ark of the Covenant was symbolic of God's throne and presence. The Tabernacle was built to house the Ark of the Covenant. The Ark was the first item of furniture constructed after God told Moses to build the Tabernacle. (Exodus 25:10–22)

The Ark of the Covenant was intended to be the central focus of the Most Holy Place in the Tabernacle and later the Temple. (Exodus 40:1–21)

The Ark of the Covenant rested in the Most Holy Place and both were separated from the rest of the Holy Place by a curtain (veil). (Exodus 26:31–33) This is the place where God spoke to the High Priest.

God set apart the tribe of Levi to carry the Ark and stand before Him to serve Him and bless His Name. (Deuteronomy 10:8)

Only the High Priest was allowed to enter the Holy of Holies once a year (Leviticus 16), on Yom Kippur, the Day of Atonement, to sacrifice and to sprinkle blood on the Mercy Seat (the area where the winged Cherubim face each other) to atone for the sins of the people. (Exodus 37:6–9)

Dimensions of the Ark: 44" long, 26.4" wide, 26.4" high. The carrying poles were 15 feet long.

The contents of the Ark are listed in Hebrews 9:4:
A jar of manna
Aaron's rod (which budded and bore fruit)
The stone tablets with the Ten Commandments

Only the tablets, as the contents of the Ark, are mentioned in Exodus 25:16 and Deut. 10:5.

All three items were reminders of the Jews wandering in the wilderness for 40 years, and were symbols of God's care for them. Each item was also a picture of the coming Messiah, Jesus.

The jar of manna reminded the people of God's constant provision. (Exodus 16)

Aaron's rod illustrated God's power of life and death. The rod that Aaron had carried was a dead tree branch, but it not only budded, it bore fruit! (Exodus 7:8–13)

The stone tablets with the Ten Commandments, written by God's own hand, were to remind the people of God's protection. (Exodus 10:1–17)

The Journey of the Ark

1. Exodus 25—God gives Moses directions to build the ark of the covenant.
2. Exodus 26:31–33—The veil is woven.
3. Exodus 40:1–21—The ark in the Tabernacle.
4. Leviticus 16; Numbers 4, 10, 14; Deuteronomy 10— The ark is carried for 40 years in wilderness.

Exodus 16:33–34 — *Manna* laid before the Testimony.

Numbers 17:8, 10 — Aaron's rod laid before the Testimony.

5. Joshua 3—Priests carry the ark across the Jordan River.

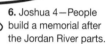

7. Joshua 6 —The ark is carried around Jericho.

6. Joshua 4—People build a memorial after the Jordan River parts.

8. Joshua 8—After conquering the town of Ai, the covenant was remembered at Mt. Ebal.

9. Joshua 18:1—Tabernacle at Shiloh.

10. Judges 20:27—Ark taken to Bethel.

11. 1 Samuel 1:3, 3:3—The LORD speaks to the child Samuel who is sleeping near the ark at Shiloh.

13. 1 Samuel 6—The Philistines return the ark to Beth Shemesh.

12. 1 Samuel 4— Philistines take the ark of God.

14. 1 Samuel 6:19–21— Men struck dead by the LORD for looking into the ark.

15. 1 Samuel 7—Ark brought to the house of Abinadab in Kiriath Jearim. It stays there 20 years.

16. 1 Samuel 14:18—Saul brings the ark to war camp temporarily.

17. 2 Samuel 6—Ark moved on a cart to the house of Obed-Edom for three months. Uzzah is struck dead.

19. 2 Samuel 15—David flees Jerusalem with the ark but sends it back to Jerusalem.

18. 2 Samuel 6:12–17—David brings the ark to Jerusalem and places it in a tent that is set up for it.

20. 1 Kings 8— Solomon has ark brought into Most Holy Place in the Temple.

21. 2 Chronicles 34:14–35:3 —Josiah recovers book of the Law and puts ark in Temple.

Scholars believe that when the Babylonians destroyed Jerusalem (586 BC), and plundered the Temple, the ark was probably taken by Nebuchadnezzar and destroyed, or hidden by Levites. Its existence, or location, remains uncertain today.

22. Jeremiah 3:16,17—Prophecy of Jeremiah that the ark would not be thought of or missed nor will another be made. It will be replaced by the LORD's presence.

Hebrews 9:11–12—When Christ came as high priest of the good things that are already here, he went through the greater and more perfect Tabernacle that is not man-made, that is to say, not a part of this creation. He did not enter by means of the blood of goats and calves; but he entered the Most Holy Place once for all by his own blood, having obtained eternal redemption. (NIV)

Revelation 11:19—Then God's temple in heaven was opened, and within his temple was seen the ark of his covenant. And there came flashes of lightning, rumblings, peals of thunder, an earthquake and a great hailstorm. (NIV)

The Tabernacle Workbook

① The Bronze Altar
Read Ex. 27:1-8

Size:
7 ½ ft. long x
7 ½ ft. wide x
4 ½ ft. high
2.3 m x 2.3 m x 1.3 m

God wanted to dwell among his people. How does a holy God dwell among sinful people? First God required the people to sacrifice a perfect animal for their sins (Lev. 17:11). The blood of the animal was important to justify the people before God. Only the finest animal—a perfect one—was good enough. Sacrifices needed to be offered on a regular basis (Heb. 9:25).

The person bringing the offering would put his hand on the head of the lamb while it was killed. This symbolically put the person's sins onto the animal, and the animal died in his place.

To think about:
• Jesus is our perfect sacrifice and shed his blood for our sins. (See John 1:29, Rev. 13:8, Hebrews 10:10, Romans 4:25.) Jesus was not only the perfect sacrifice, but his sacrifice covered all sin—past and future. No more sacrifices are required.

• In Romans 12:1, we are told to present our bodies as a living sacrifice. What does this mean to you?

② The Bronze Laver
Read Ex. 30:18 & Ex. 38:8

Size:
None
indicated

The next step was for the priests only. In fact, the rest of the work was performed by the priests on behalf of the people.

After making the sacrifice, the priest washed himself at the bronze laver. This washing purified the priest and prepared him to enter the Tabernacle. In Exodus 30:20, God says they must wash so that they do not die when they enter the Tabernacle.

The bronze laver was made from brass mirrors donated by the women. The Bible does not describe the laver completely, but perhaps it had a shiny mirrored surface which would help the priest wash thoroughly and to remind him that the Lord sees past the outward appearance, straight into the heart.

To think about:
• 1 John 1:8-9 reads: "If we claim to be without sin, we deceive ourselves and the truth is not in us. If we confess our sins, he is faithful and just and will forgive us our sins and purify us from all unrighteousness." How would Jesus' disciples understand this verse?

③ The Golden Candlestick (Lampstand)
Read Ex. 25:31-40 & Ex. 26:35

Size:
Dimensions
are unknown

From the laver, the priest passed through a veil into the Holy Place. The room he entered had three objects: a golden candlestick on the south, a table on the north and an altar of incense to the west just before the veil to the most holy place, the Holy of Holies.

The unique candlestick was beaten from a single piece of gold. It was not pieced together. Scripture tells us it was fueled by oil, not wax. It had lamps at the top of each branch, not candles.

Its purpose was to provide light in this otherwise dark room. Trimming the lamp wicks to keep them burning brightly was an important job for the priest.

To think about:
• Jesus called himself the light of the world in many places in the Bible. See John 12:46.

• Christians are called to be lights. See Acts 13:47. How are we lights?

④ The Table of Showbread
Read Ex. 25:23-30

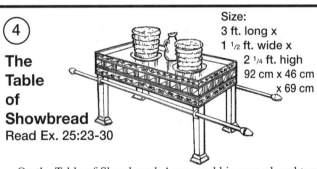

Size:
3 ft. long x
1 ½ ft. wide x
2 ¼ ft. high
92 cm x 46 cm
x 69 cm

On the Table of Showbread, Aaron and his sons placed twelve loaves of bread made from fine flour. These twelve loaves represented the twelve tribes of Israel. The table with the loaves was a continual reminder of the everlasting promises, the covenant between God and the children of Israel, and a memorial of God's provision of food. The bread was eaten by Aaron and his sons and was replaced every week on the Sabbath.

To think about:
• Jesus called himself the "Bread of Life." See John 6:35 and 6:51. He said that those who came to him would never hunger again. Physical bread—even the special bread of the Tabernacle—is consumed. But the spiritual Bread of Life, Jesus, gives eternal life.

• Hebrews 8:6-7 and Hebrews 10:16 tell of a better covenant through Jesus, one superior to the Old Testament covenant to Israel. The law would be written on people's hearts, not on tablets of stone.

(5) The Altar of Incense
Read Ex. 30:1-10

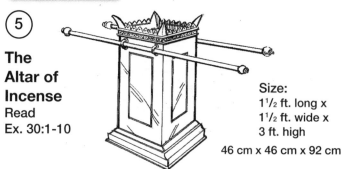

Size:
1½ ft. long x
1½ ft. wide x
3 ft. high
46 cm x 46 cm x 92 cm

The Lord required that special incense be burned constantly on the altar of incense. It was a special sweet incense, a mixture of spices to be used only for the Tabernacle. See Ex. 30:35-37. God specifically required this recipe. None other was to be burned on the altar. It was a matter of life and death, as Lev. 10:1-2 clearly shows us, when two of Aaron's sons offered a "strange fire" before the Lord and were struck dead. In the New Testament (Luke 1:5-13), the priest Zacharias was in the Holy Place when an angel appeared near the Altar of Incense. Zacharias fell down with fear. The angel announced that God had heard Zacharias's prayers and he and his wife would have a son (John the Baptist).

To think about:
• Incense represents the prayers of the faithful. There are several references to this in the book of Revelation (5:8, 8:3-4).
• Are our prayers a sweet incense toward God?

(6) The Veil
Read Ex. 26:33; Ex. 30:10

Size:
At least 15 ft. (4.6 m) wide

The Veil (sometimes spelled *vail*) separated the holy place from the most holy place where the Ark of the Covenant was kept. It was a barrier between God and man. Once a year Aaron would enter the most holy place (Holy of Holies) through this veil. The veil was a heavy woven cloth stretching for ten cubits (15 feet or 4.6 meters). There was no separation in the middle. The high priest had to go around the side to enter the most holy place.

Later when the Temple was constructed, it followed a similar design. The veil of the Temple was torn from top to bottom when Jesus died. This symbolizes the ability of every believer, not just a high priest, to approach God through the death of Jesus.

To think about:
• For hundreds of years, the Israelites needed a human high priest to represent them before God. Read 1 Timothy 2:5, Hebrews 8:1, Hebrews 9:11, and Hebrews 10:11-12. Name a few ways in which Jesus is a better high priest than Aaron.

(7) The Ark of the Covenant and the Mercy Seat

Read Ex. 25:10,14-16; Ex. 25:22; Heb. 9

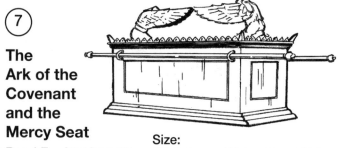

Size:
3¾ ft. long x 2¼ ft. wide x 2¼ ft. high 1.15 m x 69 cm x 69 cm

The central focus of the entire Tabernacle was the most holy place where God spoke to the high priest above the Mercy Seat—the area where the winged cherubim face each other.

Annually the high priest would sprinkle blood on the Mercy Seat to atone for the sins of all the people.

God's purpose and desire is to dwell among his people and to commune with them. The layout of the Tabernacle, along with the steps of sacrifice, cleansing, and remembering God's promises are all designed to bring sinful mankind to a loving and holy God.

To think about:
• Christianity is not a religion in which man reaches to know God. It is God who approaches his creatures and makes it possible for them to know him. (John 6:44, Eph. 2:8-9)
• Our efforts to be "good people" are not enough to approach God. Jesus alone is the Way to God. (John 14:6, Heb. 10:19-23)

Israelites Communed with God through the Tabernacle	Christians Commune with God through Jesus
1. Bronze Altar for sacrifices	Christ's sacrifice
2. Bronze Laver for washing	Cleansing through confession
3. Candlestick/Lampstand	Enlighted by the Holy Spirit
4. Table of Showbread	Fed by the Living Word
5. Altar of Incense	Prayer, communication, intercession
6-7. Through the Veil into the Most Holy Place	Entering God's presence boldly through Christ
8. Priests and the garments	Service to God and others

Why Is the Tabernacle Important Today?

1. Today, _we_ are God's dwelling place. (1 Cor. 6:19)
2. God's holy presence is among us. (Exodus 40:34-38)
3. As believers, we are part of a priesthood. (1 Peter 2:5,9, Rev. 5:10, Rev. 20:6, and Hebrews 4:16)
4. The Tabernacle shows a pattern of worship prescribed by God. (Hebrews 10:19-25)

Pattern of Worship

Write the furnishings of the Tabernacle in the order that reflects the pattern of worship Israel needed to take in order to approach God. When finished, transfer the letters to the lines below in order to decipher a verse of praise and worship from the Psalms.
The same number represents the same letter throughout the code.

1. __ __ __ __   (John 10:9)
   1 2 3 4

2. __ __ __ __ __ __   __ __ __ __ __   (Exodus 27:1-2)
   5 6 7 8 9 4   2 10 3 2 6

3. __ __ __ __ __ __   __ __ __ __ __   (Exodus 30:17-18)
   5 6 7 8 9 4   10 2 11 4 6

4. __ __ __ __ __ __   __ __ __ __ __ __ __ __ __   (Exodus 25:31)
   1 7 10 12 4 8   10 2 13 14 15 3 2 8 12

5. __ __ __ __ __   __ __   __ __ __ __ __ __ __ __ __   (Exodus 25:30)
   3 2 5 10 4   7 16   15 17 7 18 5 6 4 2 12

6. __ __ __ __ __   __ __   __ __ __ __ __ __ __   (Exodus 30:1)
   2 10 3 2 6   7 16   19 8 20 4 8 15 4

7. __ __ __ __   (Exodus 26:31)
   11 4 19 10

8. __ __ __ __ __ __ __ __   and   __ __ __ __ __   __ __ __ __ __
   20 17 4 6 21 5 19 13   13 4 6 20 22   15 4 2 3
   (Exodus 37:6-7)

__ __ __   __ __ __ __ __ __   __ __   __ __ __ __
17 7 18   10 7 11 4 10 22   19 15   22 7 21 6

__ __ __ __ __ __ __ __   __ __ __ __ __ , __   __ __ __ __ __
12 18 4 10 10 19 8 1   14 10 2 20 4   7   10 7 6 12

__ __ __ __ __ __ __ __ ! __ __ __ __ __ __
2 10 13 19 1 17 3 22   13 22 15 7 21 10

__ __ __ __ __ __ , __ __ __ __   __ __ __ __ __ __ __ ,
22 4 2 6 8 15   4 11 4 8   16 2 19 8 3 15

__ __ __   __ __ __   __ __ __ __ __ __   __ __   __ __ __
16 7 6   3 17 4   20 7 21 6 3 15   7 16   3 17 4

__ __ __ __ ; __ __   __ __ __ __ __ __   __ __ __ __ __ __
10 7 6 12   13 22   17 4 2 6 3   2 8 12 13 22

__ __ __ __ __   __ __ __   __ __ __   __ __ __ __
16 10 4 15 17   20 6 22   7 21 3   16 7 6 3 17 4

__ __ __ __ __ __   __ __ __ .
10 19 11 19 8 1   1 7 12

The Ten commandments
Exodus 20:1-17

1. Unscramble the words in italics and fill in answer on the dotted lines.
2. Fill in the missing words on the solid lines.
3. Fill in the commandment number on the line before the statement.

_____ You shall not *eumiss* .... the _____ of the Lord your God.

_____ *roohn* .... your_____ and your _____.

_____ You _____ _____ *least* ....

_____ You _____ _____ *voect* ....

_____ You shall have _____ _____ gods *ferobe* .... me.

_____ Remember the _____ _____ by *peegink* .... it holy.

_____ You _____ _____ commit *yeartuld* ....

_____ You _____ _____ give *sealf* .... testimony.

_____ You _____ _____ *rrudem*

....

_____ You shall not make for *sourflye* ....

an _____ .

This drawing illustrates two stone tablets, inscribed with the first ten characters of the Hebrew alphabet, representing the numbers 1 through 10. The Hebrew language is read right to left so the letter aleph (A) is the top character on the tablet on the right. Read from top bottom then read the left tablet from top to bottom.

Read Exodus 28:4–41

■ Consider the description of the clothing for the High Priest. Then color the drawing.

■ Write a word or two about the special significance for:

Ephod (Exodus 28:6–8)

_____

_____

Onyx stones (Exodus 28:9–14)

_____

_____

Breastplate (Exodus 28:15–21)

_____

_____

Urim and Thummim (Exodus 28:30)

_____

_____

Robe (Exodus 28:31–35)

_____

_____

Turban (Exodus 28:36–39)

_____

_____

Tunic (Exodus 28:39)

_____

_____

Sash (Exodus 28:39)

_____

_____

Turban with gold plate

IDEA
Make a breastplate or dress up as the High Priest for this lesson.

Onyx stones

Ephod

Breastplate with Urim and Thummim

Sash

Robe

Bells and Pomegranates alternate

Tunic

The High Priest

The High Priest's Breastplate

The twelve tribes of Israel and descriptions of the twelve stones Color in stones lightly with crayons.

ZEBULUN Beryl light red	ISSACHAR Topaz yellow	JUDAH Ruby dark red
GAD Diamond gray	SIMEON Sapphire blue	REUBEN Emerald green
BENJAMIN Amethyst purple	MANASSEH Agate gray striped	EPHRAIM Jacinth orange
NAPHTALI Jasper brown	ASHER Onyx black	DAN Chrysolite blue–green

The Ephod

Two onyx stones, inscribed with the names of the twelve sons of Jacob, were set in gold and fastened to the shoulder pieces of the ephod.

Reuben
Simeon
Levi
Judah
Zebulun
Issachar

Dan
Gad
Asher
Naphtali
Joseph
Benjamin

Priests and Levites

The Tribe of Levi was chosen by God to be set apart for religious service. The Torah describes their duties.

The priests (Kohanim) were a special group of Levites. They were descendants of Aaron, Israel's first High Priest.

The priests offered sacrifice on Israel's behalf. The Levites took care of the Tabernacle.

The stones on the breastplate bore the names of the twelve tribes of Israel. They were not exactly the same as the twelve sons of Jacob. Neither Levi nor Joseph had a tribe named for them. Two tribes were named for Joseph's two sons, Manasseh and Ephraim, bringing the total tribes to 12, the same as the number of Jacob's sons.

The breastplate bearing the precious stones was worn over the High Priest's heart.

Onyx stones have a translucent and opaque marbled quality and come in shades of white, cream, and natural earth tones.

No complete description of design of the urim and thummim or how they were used are given in Scripture.

The High Priest in the Old Testament

The first High Priest was Aaron, the brother of Moses. It was to be an inherited office, passed on through his sons.

The books of Leviticus, Numbers, and Deuteronomy contain detailed instructions for the duties of the High Priests and the other priests serving in the Tabernacle.

The Old Testament books of Joshua, Judges, Samuel, Kings, Chronicles and many of the Prophets record the activities of the priests and the High Priests throughout history.

LEVITES

Numbers 8:5–26 describes the setting apart of the Levites, and chapter 18 describes the duties of the Priests and Levites.

One of the special duties of the Levites was to carry the Ark of the Covenant: Joshua 3:3; 1 Samuel 6:15, 2 Samuel 15:24; 1 Kings 8:4.

Jesus Our High Priest

The Levitical Priests served temporarily, but Jesus is our Priest forever. The writer of Hebrews assures us that because Jesus lives forever, he has a permanent priesthood and is able to save completely those who come to God through him. (Hebrews 7:24–25)

The High Priest in the New Testament

In the Gospels, the High Priest is mentioned as presiding over the plot, arrest, and inquisition of Jesus prior to his crucifixion.

Priests are mentioned when Jesus healed the lepers and sent them to the priest to be declared clean. (Matthew 8; Mark 1)

Zechariah was named as a priest serving in the Temple. (Luke 1:5–25) Jesus included a priest in the Parable of the Good Samaritan. (Luke 10)

The High Priest listened to charges against the Apostles and granted Saul an arrest warrant for Christians. (Acts 4; 5; 7; 9) The High Priest listened to Paul's testimony. (Acts 22—25)

The book of Hebrews is full of references to Jesus as our High Priest. (Hebrews 2:17; 3:1; 4:14–15; 5:10; 6:19–20; 9:11)

Jesus, Our High Priest

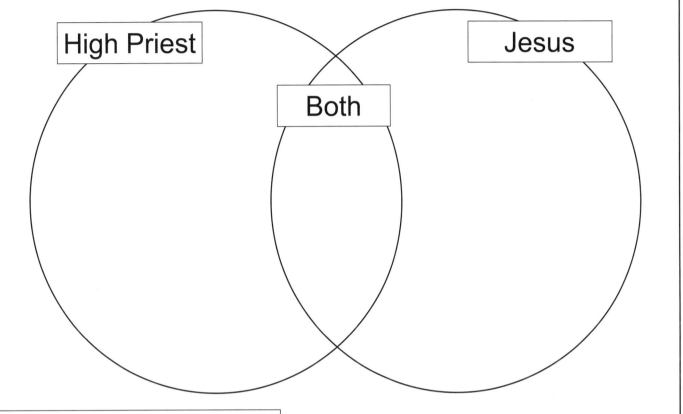

High Priests in the Old Testament served God in the Tabernacle and later in the Temple. In the New Testament, the book of Hebrews refers to Jesus Christ our High Priest. Using the list of traits below, write the ones that are unique to the High Priest in one circle. Write the ones that are unique to Jesus Christ in the other circle. In the middle, write the traits that they both possess.

Human

God

Chosen by God

Sinner

Holy

Died

Died and rose again

Served as intermediary for people

Sacrificed for his own sin and for the sin of the people

Sacrificed for all people for all time

Seated with God

Entered God's presence once a year

Begged for forgiveness

Had the power to forgive sin

Sent the Holy Spirit

Savior

Authority on earth

Authority in heaven and earth

JESUS IN THE TEMPLE

Jesus never physically set foot in the Tabernacle. It was replaced by the Temple in Jerusalem about 1,000 years before his birth.

The Bible records Jesus' visits to the Temple beginning with the first week of his life on earth and ending with the week of his death.

Every recorded visit demonstrated his deity and his mission as Messiah. Anna and Simeon recognized him as Messiah and the teachers in the Temple were amazed at his godly wisdom.

■ Choose one or more of the Bible verses below and draw pictures illustrating Jesus in the Temple.

Dedicated as an infant: Luke 2:22–38
Talking to the teachers: Luke 2:41–52
The Feast of Tabernacles: John 7
The Feast of Dedication (Chanukah): John 10:22–23
Widow's Mite: Mark 12:41–44; Luke 21:1–4
The Money Changers: Matthew 21:12–17
Predicting the Destruction: Luke 21:5–6

Symbols and Salvation

The parts of the Tabernacle seen in Jesus Christ and the followers of Christ

TABERNACLE	SCRIPTURE	JESUS CHRIST	FOLLOWERS OF CHRIST
Gate	John 10:1–18 John 14:6	Shepherd, The Gate Way, Truth, Life	Belief, Faith
Blood Sacrifice	John 1:29 2 Corinthians 5:7	"This is my body. . ." Crucifixion and Resurrection	Cross
Water Basin	John 7	Living Water	Baptism
Lampstand	John 8:12	Light of the World	Witness
Bread Table	John 3:32–35	Bread of Life	Communion or "Lord's Supper" Table, Bible
Incense/Prayer	Matthew 2:9–11 John 17	Jesus' Prayer (John 17) Lord's Prayer (Matt. 6:5–15)	Prayer
Mercy Seat	Luke 22:17–20	Last Supper Way to the Father	Communion or "Lord's Supper"

GATE

Jesus called himself the "gate for the sheep" and the "good shepherd." (John 10) He said, "I am the way, the truth, and the life." (John 14:6)

BLOOD SACRIFICE

The crucifixion and resurrection were central to Jesus' life and ministry. He said, "This cup is the new covenant in my blood, which is poured out for you." (Luke 22:20) Christian churches often display crosses to proclaim the crucifixion and resurrection as the central point of their faith.

LIGHT

Jesus said he was the "Light of the World" (John 8:12), and celebrated Chanukah, the Festival of Light. (John 10:22–23)

WATER

Jesus was baptized in water. (Mark 1:9) Jesus promised the Samaritan woman living water (John 4:13–14), and he promised it to all at the Feast of Tabernacles. (John 7:38)

Christians follow Jesus' example and command in baptism.

INCENSE PRAYER

Many of Jesus' teachings on the importance of prayer are recorded in the Bible. Prayer is central to the worship of God.

BREAD

Jesus said he was the "Bread of Life." (John 3:32–35) On the night Jesus was betrayed, he took bread, gave thanks and broke it, and gave it to his disciples, saying, "This is my body given for you; do this in remembrance of me." (Luke 22:19)

Today followers of Christ eat bread during Holy Communion in remembrance of Jesus and his sacrifice on the cross.

MERCY

The Mercy Seat was a preview of Jesus' blood sacrifice to wash away our sin. (John 3:16) The Apostle Paul wrote about repentance and God's great mercy and grace. (Eph. 2:4–10)

JESUS IS . . .

Look up the verses and fill in the blanks.

Jesus is the _____
(John 10:7,9)

Jesus is the _____
(Luke 22:20)

Jesus is the _____
(John 4:14)

Jesus is the _____
(John 8:12)

Jesus is the _____
(John 6:35)

Jesus is the _____
(John 10:11)

Jesus is the _____
(John 14:6)

Jesus is the _____
(John 15:5)

SCRIPTURE

Leviticus 23

JOURNEY INFORMATION

God made a way for his people to remember their history and blessings. (Leviticus 23) He created a system of feasts and holidays around the annual harvests, four holidays in the spring and three in the fall.

Passover, Unleavened Bread and First Fruits occur in March or April and Pentecost 50 days after Passover. Rosh HaShanah, Yom Kippur and Sukkot are the fall holidays. Chanukah and Purim, winter celebrations, were added later.

Jesus' life and sacrifice are illustrated in each of the Jewish Feasts.

YOM KIPPUR
Leviticus 23:26–32

The Day of Atonement was the annual recognition of their sins by the people of God. The High Priest entered the Holy of Holies with a blood sacrifice to beg God for forgiveness.

Jesus was the final atonement for all people, for all time. Through his sacrifice we can approach God to ask for forgiveness.

HEBREW FEASTS & HOLY DAYS

Pesach (pronounced PAY–sahk) means to "pass over."

Yom Kippur (pronounced Yome Ki–POOR) means "day of atonement" or "day of covering."

Sukkot (pronounced SOO–KOTE) means to "cover over." The Hebrew word *sukkah* refers to a temporary shelter, also referred to as a booth, or a tabernacle.

Chanukah (pronounced with a hard, guttural "h" at the beginning KHA–noo–kah) means "dedication."

PESACH (PASSOVER)
Leviticus 23:4–5, Exodus 12:1–14

Passover and Unleavened Bread combine to create an 8–day celebration. Passover looks back and remembers how God saved his people from slavery in Egypt and the night the Angel of Death "passed over" the homes with sacrificial blood on their doorpost. Passover also looks forward to the sacrificial blood of Jesus with its power to save us from our sin. Only matzah is eaten during the eight days in remembrance of the unleavened bread eaten by the Jews as they fled Egypt. Jesus celebrated Passover with his disciples. Christian Holy Communion is based on the bread and wine. (Luke 22:7–20)

CHANUKAH

The Feast of Dedication is mentioned in the Bible when Jesus celebrated it in Jerusalem. (John 10:22) Information about Chanukah is found in the Jewish book of Macabees.

Chanukah is also known as the Feast of Dedication and the Festival of Lights. The 8–day celebration recalls how the Jews rescued the Temple in 165 AD. After cleansing it from the desecration of their enemies, they rededicated the Temple. God gave the Jews a great miracle. They only had one day's worth of sacramental oil to relight the flame in the Temple, yet it burned for eight days while new oil was being purified. Chanukah reminds us of God's faithfulness and Jesus' announcement that he was the Light of the World. (John 8:12)

FEASTS and HOLIDAYS
Refer to Rose chart 446L for details about Feasts of the Bible.

SUKKOT
Leviticus 23:33–43

Commonly called the Feast of Tabernacles or the Feast of Booths, Sukkot is the annual fall harvest festival. God commanded his people to construct and live in temporary shelters in remembrance of their temporary home for 40 years in the wilderness. Sukkot was one of the pilgrimage holidays faithful Jews were commanded to celebrate in Jerusalem.

Sukkot is connected to Passover by its focus on life in the wilderness following the escape from slavery in Egypt.

Sukkot is also connected to Chanukah and the rededication of the Temple because it was the holiday celebrated by King Solomon when the Temple was first dedicated.

Jesus traveled to Jerusalem to celebrate Sukkot. While there he taught in the Temple courts. (John 7)

ACTIVITIES
Plan to set up your classroom and celebrate one of the Jewish holidays. See Rose wall chart 446L for more details on the holidays.

For **Sukkot** you could construct a simple sukkah (an arbor) using two step–ladders for the walls and placing real or twisted paper branches across the top. The roof and walls should not be solid. Drape the roof and sides with artificial fruit and leaves. Have your class sit inside the sukkah for the lesson. Fresh fruit would be an appropriate snack.

For **Passover** you could set up your classroom and enact a seder. The seder meal is the annual celebration remembering the first passover (Exodus 12:1–14). Christians and Jews celebrate Passover. (Instructions for preparing a seder with information pointing out how Jesus is evident in the celebration are available in Christian book–stores.) Prepare a sample seder plate containing the special food used during the Passover celebration to share with the students. Matzah and grape juice would be a good snack.

For **Chanukah** you could tell the story of the rededication of the Temple and the miracle of the oil. Make a simple menorah (8–branch candelabra) and light the candles, play the dreidl game and serve donuts and latkes (potato pancakes) for snacks.

Feasts, Fun, and Facts

JOURNEY INFORMATION

■ **CHILDREN OF ISRAEL**
God's people are often called the "children of Israel" even though they are not all children.

■ **THE WILDERNESS**
The Sinai Peninsula where Mt. Sinai is located is sometimes referred to as "the wilderness."

■ **THE PROMISED LAND**
Roughly the area between the Jordan River and the Mediterranean Sea, from Syria to Egypt, is called the "Promised Land." This is a reference to the promise that God made to Abraham many years earlier.

GOD'S CARE FOR HIS PEOPLE

■ God chose Moses to lead His people out of bondage in Egypt to the Promised Land. Their route took them into the wilderness of Sinai (Numbers 9:1, 5–23) where they wandered for 40 years because of their grumbling and disobedience. His children may not have been faithful, but God was. He provided for them in the wilderness while he taught and tested them.

ACTIVITY

■ Read three or more of these Scripture passages about Moses and the children of srael. Write a short sentence about how God cared for them and cares for us today.

Moses: Exodus 2

Deliverance: Exodus 14:29–31   God provided a miraculous escape from Egypt.

Bread and Meat: Exodus 16:4–5, 13–17, 21–22, 31, 33–35   God provided for his people.

Water: Numbers 20:1–13

Twelve Spies: Numbers 13:26–30   God desires to give his people great gifts.

Offerings: Numbers 15:17–21   God allows his people to give back to him.

Balaam's Donkey: Numbers 22:21–38; 24:1–13   God uses unexpected ways to protect his people.

Feasts/Holidays: Numbers 28:16–29:40   God's gift of holidays and feast days are constant reminders of his blessings.

Blessing: Numbers 6:22–27   God's verbal blessing for his people.

Bronze Snake: Numbers 21:4–9   A wonderful preview of salvation through the Savior.

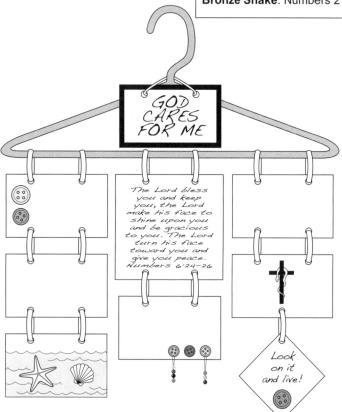

ACTIVITY

■ Create a mobile about God's care for His people. Use six to eight 3" x 5" cards. (Cut some smaller cards if desired.) Use some of the events in the Scriptures above. On one side of each card write a Bible verse, portion of a verse, or personal response. On the other side draw an illustration of God's care for his people.

Punch holes in the cards so they will hang vertically, horizontally or diagonally, and thread yarn or ribbon through the holes. Attach two or three cards to a coat hanger. Attach the remaining cards to each other. Slip one card through the hook at the top of the hanger and write "God Cares for Me" on it.

If you like, glue buttons, beads, small stones, seashells, or other materials to several of the cards.

Hang your mobile where it will remind you that God cares for you, or give it to someone who needs God's care.

OPTIONS:

■ Create 3" x 5" cards as above and store in a card file box. Review cards for daily devotions and prayer time.

■ Create 3" x 5" cards, decorating only one side. Laminate and glue a small magnet on the blank side. Display the cards on a refrigerator or other metal surface.

■ *Aron* is the word used for the Ark of the Covenant. It is also translated "chest." Other references include:
Ark of Testimony (Exodus 25:22)
Ark of the Covenant (Numbers 10:33)
Ark of God (1 Samuel 3:3)
Ark of the Lord God (1 Kings 2:26)
Holy Ark (2 Chronicles 35:3)
Ark of Thy Strength (Psalm 132:8)

■ The word *ark* is mentioned over 200 times in the Bible. About 30 times, it is in reference to Noah's Ark.

■ Translated, *manna* means "What is it?"

■ Instructions for moving the Ark include covering it with a porpoise skin. (Numbers 4:5–6)

■ The Tabernacle and the Ark remained at Shiloh from Joshua 18 to 1 Samuel 4.

■ The last time the Ark is "seen" as recorded in Scripture is 2 Chronicles 35:3. There is speculation that the Ark disappeared during the Babylonian captivity.

■ Jeremiah predicted that Israel would lose the Ark, and that they wouldn't even care! (Jeremiah 3:16)

■ Zechariah was struck dumb as he burned incense in the Temple. He couldn't speak until his son, John (the Baptist), was born. (Luke 1:5–23, 57–64)

■ The carrying poles for the Ark stuck out beyond the veil. (1 Kings 8:8)

■ In Jewish synagogues today, the cupboard where the scrolls of the Law are kept is called the Ark.

■ The recipe for the holy anointing oil is found in Exodus 30:22–26.

■ The recipe for the only incense to be burned in the Tabernacle is found in Exodus 30:34–38.

■ Wax was not used for candles until Roman times.

■ The Israelites were not alone in the wilderness. There were many populated cities and towns.

■ The Book of Numbers is about more than the census.

■ The word *tabernacle* means "to dwell."

■ *Tabernacle* is most often used as a noun, but occasionally it is used as a verb. To "tabernacle" with God means to dwell with him.

■ In some translations, the word *tabernacle* is used for the structures Peter suggested building in Matthew 17:4, Mark 9:5, and Luke 9:33.

■ *Tabernacle* is mentioned over 300 times in the Old Testament and 25 times in the New Testament. Most of the time it is speaking about the Tabernacle, but a few verses refer to the Feast of Tabernacles or to a dwelling.

■ Sukkot, the Feast of Tabernacles, or the Feast of Booths, is the fall harvest celebration.

■ The celebration of Thanksgiving is based on the Feast of Tabernacles.

■ The priests were permitted to eat the meat from some of the burnt sacrifices as well as the bread in the Holy Place. Processing the olive oil for the lamps on the Temple took 8 days. The Feast of Dedication, also known as Chanukah, began in 165 BC when one day's oil miraculously burned for 8 days until new oil was ready.

■ Jesus celebrated Chanukah. (John 10:22–23)

■ Jesus celebrated the Feast of Tabernacles. (John 7:1–16)

■ The Feast of Tabernacles, Sukkot, is the 7th feast of the year lasting 7 days, and it is in the 7th month. (Leviticus 23:33–43)

■ The last time the Tabernacle is mentioned in Scripture is in the Book of Revelation.

■ The term *scapegoat* comes from the practice of sending the scapegoat into the wilderness to bear away the sins of the people on Yom Kippur.

■ David fed himself and his army with the bread on the Table of Showbread in the Tabernacle when they were on the run from King Saul.

■ Aaron's sons died when they burned strange incense in the Tabernacle.

■ The Feast of Tabernacles is one of the three required annual feasts.

■ By Jesus' time, the role of the High Priest was a political position.

■ *Bethlehem* means "house of bread."

■ According to Jewish tradition, the veils in Herod's Temple were so heavy it took 300 priests to hang them.

■ We remember Israel's priestly line today in familiar Jewish names such as Levi and Levine.

■ Two different Hebrew words are translated *ark* in Scripture: *tebáh* and *aron*. *Tebáh* is the word used in referring to Noah's Ark. It is translated "basket" when telling of the "ark" used to save baby Moses. Both of these arks were sealed inside and out, both were intended to float, and both were intended to save life.

MY CALENDAR OF WORSHIP

Use this worksheet to design a personal calendar to help remember God's presence and blessings.

God instructed Moses to construct the Tabernacle so that the people would have a visible reminder of God's presence with them. He wanted to be their only God, their protector, and their teacher. In response, God desired their sincere worship. In addition to the Tabernacle, God also gave the children of Israel a calendar of holiday and feast days in order to praise God as well as make it easy

and exciting to remember God's blessings. Photocopy this calendar, fill in the blank squares with your own ideas on how to experience God's presence each day, and then use it to help remind you to worship, thank and praise God daily. There are no numbers on the days, so you can use this calendar over and over again.

Imagine a week with only three days or one with 13! Thank God for creating the perfect week.			Consider what holidays are coming up this month and plan a celebration that thanks God.			
		Say a prayer before you eat. Remember that all food is a blessing from God.			Read Psalm 23 or 139 several times and write down the key words that tell you God wants to be part of your life.	
	Give some of your own money to a missionary who tells others how much God wants to be in their life.			Draw an outline around your hand. Inside write a list of ways you can help others know that God loves them.		
		Thank God for your wonderful brain. How can you use it to honor Him?			Evaluate the games you play and the movies you watch. Do they honor God?	
	Write a note to a family member or friend and tell them how you see God in their life and actions.			Pick a person in the Bible you would like to talk to. How would you explain our life and times today to him or her?		

You Are There

Teacher reference to the Tabernacle cards (page 32)

Progressing through the Tabernacle following the path of the priest can help students understand God's plan for worship.

FLOOR DRAWING OF TABERNACLE

Begin by creating a large drawing of the Tabernacle on the floor of your meeting room. Use a piece of butcher paper 6 feet by 3 feet and outline the Tabernacle following the drawing on page 6. Next, photocopy the Tabernacle furniture on pages 11–17 and place them on the Tabernacle drawing in the appropriate positions.

Place the Tabernacle drawing on the floor in the middle of the room. Place chairs or pillows around the edges for seating.

TABERNACLE CARDS

Photocopy the information cards (page 32), cut them apart, and pass them out to the class. If you have a large class, photocopy as many sets as needed to be sure everyone receives at least one card. It's alright if several students receive the same card or if several students receive more than one card.

HIGH PRIEST

The class leader or other volunteer may wish to dress as the High Priest (see illustration on page 23). Begin with the leader reading Exodus 29:45–46 and Psalm 122:1. Review the layout of the Tabernacle (page 6), the Path of Worship (page 38), and the clothing of the High Priest (pages 23–24).

TABERNACLE VISIT

Now, the leader is ready to begin a Tabernacle visit. As the priest approaches the Tabernacle, the student with the first card will read it for the class. Continue "walking" through the Tabernacle with students reading corresponding cards. (1-A, 1-B, 1-C, 2-A …)

There are three cards for each stop: Tabernacle, Old Testament meaning, and significance for believers today.

As the cards are read, be sure to take time to discuss the information and answer any questions. You may also want to include additional information from the Bible or from this workbook.

A Tabernacle Facts	B Old Testament and Priests	C New Testament and Today
1–A: Priests were from the tribe of Levi. They wore special clothing.	1–B: Priests ministered on behalf of the people.	1–C: Through Jesus' sacrifice we can come directly to God.
2–A: The Tabernacle wall was too high to see over, but the gate was wide enough for all to enter.	2–B: God's people were to be a separate people. There was only one way to come to God.	2–C: There is still only one way to God: salvation through Jesus Christ.
3–A: The Bronze Altar was acacia wood covered with bronze.	3–B: Sin separated humans from God and had to be dealt with. A blood sacrifice was needed.	3–C: Jesus Christ was the final blood sacrifice.
4–A: The Bronze Laver was a wash basin.	4–B: Priests needed clean hands. (Psalm 24:3–6)	4–C: Jesus' sacrifice cleanses our sin. (Titus 3:5)
5–A: White, blue, purple and red curtains represent God's special colors. Made from animal skins.	5–B: Only the priests could enter the Holy Place.	5–C: Believers can enter God's presence through Jesus Christ.
6–A: The lampstand of gold represented God's holy light. Seven may be for the days of creation.	6–B: The priests kept the oil lamps burning.	6–C: Jesus is the light of the world shining through the lives of believers.
7–A: The Table of Showbread contained food for the priests and illustrated God's provision.	7–B: The twelve loaves represented the 12 Tribes of Israel.	7–C: Jesus is the Bread of Life.
8–A: The Altar of Incense represented prayer and stood before the Veil.	8–B: Priests burned incense made from God's special recipe.	8–C: God delights in our prayers.
9–A: God's presence was hidden behind the Veil. The Veil was one piece, from ceiling to floor.	9–B: Only the High Priest could go around the Veil and enter the Holy of Holies once a year.	9–C: God demonstrated his invitation to enter his presence by tearing the Veil from top to bottom when Jesus died.
10–A: Holy of Holies, designed to hold the Ark of the Covenant. Ark: acacia wood in gold.	10–B: Ark contents: The Law – Protection Aaron's Rod – Presence Manna – Provision	10–C: Jesus sent the Holy Spirit to be God's Presence in believers. The Bible is our guide.
11–A: Lid of the Ark: Golden Cherubim and Mercy Seat. God's dwelling place.	11–B: The High Priest sprinkled blood on the Mercy Seat to atone for the sin of the people.	11–C: Jesus' blood is the final atonement. Believers may enter God's presence.

"You Are There" Tabernacle Cards

Photocopy and cut apart for student participation as your class follows the path of the High Priest in the Tabernacle.

1–A The priests and the High Priest were from the family of Aaron and the tribe of Levi. They wore special clothing.	1–B The priests ministered in the Tabernacle, and later in the Temple, before God, on behalf of the people.	1–C Jesus' sacrifice made it possible for believers to come before Almighty God without a priest to offer their prayers.
2–A The wall around the Tabernacle was made of linen. It was 7½ feet tall. The gate was 30 feet wide.	2–B The wall demonstrated that God's people were separate. The gate illustrated that there was only one way to God.	2–C Believing in Jesus Christ is the only way to be saved and the only way to God.
3–A The Bronze Altar was made of acacia wood covered with bronze. It was 7½ feet square.	3–B God takes sin very seriously. A blood sacrifice was the only way to forgive sin.	3–C Jesus was the final blood sacrifice. Now we can ask for God's forgiveness in Jesus' Name.
4–A The Bronze Laver was a wash basin mounted on a base.	4–B The priests had to wash before entering the Holy Place.	4–C Jesus' sacrifice cleanses us from sin.
5–A The Holy Place was separated from the Outer Court by a curtain of white, blue, purple, and red.	5–B The people could go into the Outer Court but only the priests could go into the Holy Place.	5–C Through Jesus' sacrifice, believers have direct access to God.
6–A The Golden Lampstand was made of one piece of gold weighing 125 pounds. It was designed to hold 7 oil lamps.	6–B A priest was to keep the oil lamps burning at all times to represent God's presence with his people.	6–C Jesus said he was the light of the world and that believers are to be God's light to others.
7–A: The Table of Showbread sat opposite the Golden Lampstand. A priest was responsible to replace the 12 loaves made from fine flour every Sabbath. The priests ate the bread.	7–B The 12 loaves represented the 12 Tribes of Israel and were a reminder that God would provide for his people.	7–C Jesus said, "I am the bread of life. He who comes to me will never go hungry, and he who believes in me will never be thirsty." (John 6:35)
8–A The Altar of Incense stood before the curtain that separated the Holy of Holies from the Holy Place. God gave a special recipe for the incense.	8–B A priest was to burn incense continually on the altar to represent the prayers of the people.	8–C God delights in the prayers of his people. They are a sweet aroma to him.
9–A The Veil was a very special item in the Tabernacle and later the Temple. It was one single piece of fabric with an embroidered design.	9–B The Veil separated God's presence in the Holy of Holies from the rest of the Tabernacle. Only the High Priest could enter once a year.	9–C: When Jesus was crucified, the Veil in the Temple tore from top to bottom. God accepted Jesus' sacrifice and now believers can go before Him in the name of Jesus without a priest.
10–A The Holy of Holies was designed to hold the Ark of the Covenant. The Ark was made of acacia wood covered in gold.	10–B The Ark contained the tablets of stone with the 10 Commandments, Aaron's rod that budded, and a jar of manna. It reminded the people of God's protection, presence, and provision.	10–C As believers, we have God's presence, the Holy Spirit, living in us. We also have the Holy Bible to assure us of God's presence, protection, and provision.
11–A Atop the Ark, the Cherubim and the Mercy Seat were made of gold to honor God's holiness and majesty. It was the place where God was pleased to dwell.	11–B The High Priest approached the Mercy Seat once a year, on Yom Kippur, and sprinkled it with the blood of a perfect sacrifice as atonement for the sin of the people.	11–C Jesus' blood represented the final perfect sacrifice. Believers don't have to wait for a priest or for one day. They may approach God personally with their prayers and praise.

Tabernacle Times

Here's your chance to publish your own newspaper. You can be a newspaper reporter, a foreign correspondent, or even the editor! Ask some friends to be contributing reporters.

● Make your own newspaper or photocopy page 34 and refer to the illustration below. To change your headline stories, cover the preprinted wording with plain paper before photocopying the page.
● Prepare by doing some research. "Interview" significant people, create interest, and draw a picture. Now start writing your stories.
● Begin your front page by indicating the date and volume number of your edition. Include a city or place name (real or fictional) and set your price.
● Follow the suggested format on this page or create your own.
● Write directly onto your photocopied page, or type your stories and then cut and paste.
● Photocopy pictures, cut and paste.

PAGE 1

■ Panel 1: Write about the Ark of the Covenant. (Refer to pages 17–18.)

■ Panels 2 & 3: This is your feature headline story. Use information from Exodus 25:8, 22 and this workbook to write an exciting story about the Tabernacle and God's presence with his people.

■ Panel 4: For reader interest, choose one or two fascinating facts. (page 29)

■ Panel 5: Choose a topic from the Tabernacle cards on page 32 and write a brief comment..

■ Panel 6: Use a graphic illustration. (See below or draw your own.)

■ Panels 7 & 8: This is your second headline. Read John 7 and write your report. An alternate second headline could be "Jesus Christ Revealed in the Tabernacle." See Hebrews 6:19–20; 7:24–8:2. (related verses: page 26 and Hebrews 3:1–6; 4:14–16)

PAGE 2

Once you've completed Page 1, you might want to think about a second page for your newspaper. Check your local newspaper for ideas.
It could be fun and challenging to include features such as (a) an Editorial, (b) Letters to the Editor, (c) a Dear Hannah advice column, (d) a Reader's Ask column, (e) the Weather, (f) Community Events, (g) a Society Column, (h) Crossword Puzzle, (i) Classified, and (j) a Market Ad. You'll probably think of lots more!

◆ For "a" and "b," choose an issue and write your personal comments about it.
◆ In "c," ask Hannah how to handle a personal issue.
◆ For "d," use a reader write–in question format and answer the question.
◆ For "e," be sure to check an almanac or the Internet to be consistent with your chosen location and date of publication for weather.
◆ For "f," create some interesting events, or report on birthdays, weddings, anniversaries, new babies, and so on.
◆ For "g," create a significant event and invite the community to participate. Check appropriate dates and report on celebrating one of the Jewish holidays. (page 27)
◆ For "h," design a simple crossword puzzle. Include the answers.
◆ For "i," write want ads, property for sale, job opportunities, and so on.
◆ For "j," design an ad for the local market.

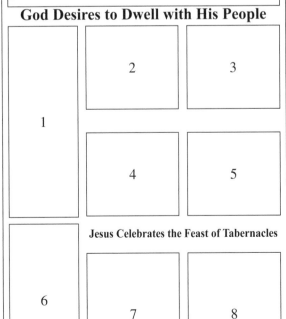

Tabernacle Times

God Desires to Dwell with His People

1	2	3
	4	5

Jesus Celebrates the Feast of Tabernacles

6	7	8

Sukkah

God Desires to Dwell with His People

Jesus Celebrates the Feast of Tabernacles

Tabernacle Details

Diagram

Fill in the blanks to label the Tabernacle. Check page 6 for information. Check page 40 for the answers.

NOTE: The outline, representing the linen curtain, is not to scale.

SIZE: _____ long by _____ wide

8. _____

7. _____
made of _____

9. _____

2. _____
made of _____

1. _____

6. _____
made of _____

3. _____
made of _____

10. _____
made of _____

5. _____
made of _____

4. _____

Read the Scripture references and complete these sentences.

NOTE: Different versions of the Bible refer to the Tabernacle as *the sanctuary, congregation,* or *tent of meeting.*

■ Exodus 40:34–38

The Tabernacle, as the Tent of Meeting, was moveable. The Israelites carried it with them as they traveled.

They knew when it was time to move because _____

_____

■ Exodus 26:33–34; 40:20–21
The Holy of Holies was the special enclosure for the _____

_____

■ Hebrews 9:4
The three things kept in the Ark were _____

_____

These three things reminded God's people of _____

_____

■ Exodus 36:8, 14, 19
The curtain walls of the Tabernacle were constructed of _____

_____

The colors of the curtain walls of the Tabernacle were _____

Tabernacle Details

Use this worksheet to explore the details of purpose, construction and travel of the Tabernacle in the wilderness.

IMPORTANCE OF DETAIL

Exodus 26–27; Exodus 35:4–37:29

God gave very specific details for the Tabernacle's construction, use, and transport.
It was a picture of his plan of salvation.

DESIGNED FOR TRAVEL

Numbers 2

The Tabernacle was the moveable tent of meeting. It could be taken down and set up in the middle of camp.

THE GLORY OF GOD

Exodus 25:8, 21–22; 40:34–38

In the Tabernacle, we can learn about God's glory. God chose to dwell with his people.
The Israelites actually saw God's glory in the cloud above the Tabernacle. The holy significance of the Tabernacle is that it was designed to contain the Ark of the Covenant and the presence of God within the Holy of Holies.

THE GLORY OF JESUS

New Testament writers saw symbolic meaning in the Tabernacle. Implied in its construction is a spiritual parallel to Christ and the church. (Matthew 27:50–51; John 1:14; Ephesians 2:19–23; Hebrews 10:19–22; 1 Peter 2:4–5)

Read Exodus 36:8–19 and write down one thing that you didn't know before reading this text.

_____

How was the presence of God seen by the people? (Exodus 40:34–38) _____

Name three animal materials used for the Tabernacle. (Exodus 26:7, 14)_____

_____

What were the outer dimensions of the Tabernacle?

(Exodus 27:18) _____

If one cubit is 18 inches (.46 meters), then the Tabernacle would measure
_____ by _____.

Follow the journey of the Tabernacle from the Sinai Peninsula to the Promised Land. Use the letters on the map to help you

Fill in the map with these place names.

> Mount Sinai
> Kibroth–hattaavah
> Hazetoth
> Ezion Geber
> Kadesh Barnea
> Ezion Geber
> Petra
> Punon
> Oboth
> Zoar
> Lu al arim
> Dibon
> Jahaz
> Heshbon
> Jericho

Check the map section in your Bible or use the one on page 40.

Enlarge map on photocopier

Review

JOURNEY INFORMATION

You and your class have come to the end of your "journey." For this final lesson on the Tabernacle, take the opportunity to review what you have learned and to complete some of the lessons or activities that you didn't include in previous classes.

QUIZ

Have students retake the Tabernacle Fact Quiz (page 8) and compare their answers with those of the first quiz they took.

Use this quiz as an opportunity to discuss new things the class has learned about the Tabernacle. Ask them what they found interesting and what was their favorite part of the Tabernacle or their favorite activity.

Q & A

Divide the class into teams of two or three. Ask each team to create four questions about the Tabernacle. Have teams take turns asking their questions to the class and allow other teams to answer.

PASSPORT

Have students complete their passports.

"AMEN"

Photocopy the script on pages 9–10. Have three students perform the skit for the class.

CALENDAR

Photocopy page 38 for each student and follow the instructions to complete the activity.

THE TABERNACLE

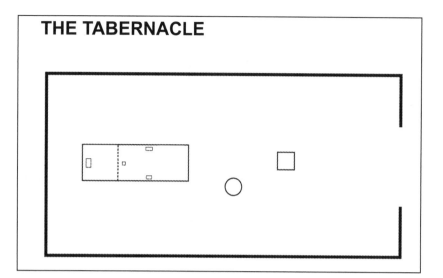

QUICK REFERENCE GUIDE

Read information from page 5 and have students take notes. Copy page 5. Students may want to keep this in their Bibles as a quick reference for the Tabernacle.

INSTANT RECALL

Photocopy the drawing of the Tabernacle (above) for each student. Challenge them to fill in as much information as they can remember about the Tabernacle in five minutes.

FASCINATING FACTS

Photocopy page 29 for each student. Have students take turns reading the fascinating facts to the class.

GOD MADE A WAY

Have students create the mobile on page 28, or add more cards to the ones that they've already made.

CELEBRATE!

Have a class party. Use the information on page 27 and Rose wall chart Feasts of the Bible (446L) to celebrate one of the Jewish holidays as a class. Decorate your room and have the students help prepare the refreshments.

MATZAH FEAST

Buy premade matzah at the grocery store. Set up a table with a variety of toppings, such as butter, jelly, fruit, frosting, sprinkles, applesauce, raisins, chopped nuts, and so on. Let students create their own snack.

JOURNEY INFORMATION

God provided the way for mankind to worship him. For many years the Tabernacle was that way. The Tabernacle, from the Hebrew word *shakhan,* means "to dwell." It represented God's presence in the middle of his people. (Exodus 29:44–46) The Tabernacle illustrated the only way sinful man could approach the Holy God. The Tabernacle and Levitical system was the method God chose to show us the right view of God and how he is to be worshipped. The pathway the priest took toward the presence of God in the Holy of Holies illustrates how God wants to be approached. (Exodus 25–27, 35–40)

God desires to dwell with his people, but he put a fence around his dwelling place. The fence represented God's holiness and righteousness, which were the two aspects that separate God and man. God provided a way for mankind to approach him by placing a gate in the fence. The gate was 30 feet wide! After entering through the gate, worship continued with repentance, cleansing, illumination, nourishment, praise, and God's mercy. The gate was a preview of Jesus who would provide the only way to God. (John 10:9; John 14:6)

ACTIVITY

Make a bookmark to remind you of God's design for worship. Photocopy the bookmark design at the right and write a favorite Bible verse on the back. You may want to use one of these verses: John 12:46; Titus 3:5; or 1 John 1:9. Paste the bookmark on cardstock or construction paper and laminate if you choose. Trim, and finish by adding a tail of ribbon or embroidery floss.

COMPARE

Before the Tabernacle, God's people worshipped him with prayer, praise, and sacrifice. Look up these verses and compare the men and worship.

Altars: Genesis 8:27; 13:18; 17:15

Prayer and praise: Genesis 20:17; Exodus 15:2; 18:9-12

Sacrifice: Genesis 46:1

Desire to worship God: Exodus 10:25-26

The Path of Worship

The Gate
The only way to approach God
Psalm 84:1–2; John 10:9

Repentance/Sacrifice
Leviticus 17:11; Hebrews 10:10

Purification
Exodus 30:20; Titus 3:5;
1 John 1:8–9

Light
Exodus 25:31–40; John 12:46

Nourishment
Exodus 25:23–30; John 6:35

Prayer and Praise
Exodus 30:35–37; Psalm 89:1–2;
Psalm 134; Revelation 8:3–4

The Veil
Exodus 26:33; 1 Timothy 2:5;
Hebrews 10:19–23

Mercy
Exodus 25:21–22; John 3:16;
John 14:6; Hebrews 10:19–23

ACTIVITY

Compare Acts 2:42 with the Tabernacle._____

_____

_____

Compare it with worship today._____

_____

_____

What things are the same? _____

_____

_____

What things are different? _____

_____

_____

Wherever you choose to worship God, you can follow this path of love, redemption and mercy.

Answers and Resources

Page 8 Quiz

1. c
2. b
3. F
4. T
5. b
6. T
7. a
8. c
9. T
10. c
11. F
12. T
13. a
14. T
15. b
16. altar of sacrifice
    bronze laver
17. golden lampstand,
    table of showbread,
    altar of incense
28. Aaron's rod, Ten
    Commandments,
    jar of manna

Page 14 The Provision of God

Deuteronomy 8:3: God provides for our physical nourishment with bread for food. He also provides for our spiritual nourishment with his Word.

1 Kings 17:8–16: In the lesson of Elijah and the widow of Zarephath, we can see that God is the provider of physical and spiritual nourishment for his people.

Matthew 6:11: In the third verse of the Lord's Prayer, Jesus reminds us that we are to recognize our daily need for food as a gift from God.

Luke 9: 10–17: Jesus provided an abundant lunch for the crowd of over 5,000 because he was concerned about their physical need for food as well as their spiritual needs. Just in case someone didn't recognize this as a miracle from God, there were 12 baskets of leftovers!

Page 21 Bible Search

1. GATE
2. BRONZE ALTAR
3. BRONZE BASIN
4. GOLDEN LAMPSTAND
5. TABLE OF SHOWBREAD
6. ALTAR OF INCENSE
7. VEIL
8. CHERUBIM and MERCY
   SEAT

How lovely is your dwelling place, O Lord Almighty! My soul yearns, even faints, for the courts of the Lord; my heart and flesh cry out for the living God.

Page 26 Jesus Is. . .

John 10:7,9:   The Gate
Luke 22:20:   The New Covenant
John 4:14:   Spring of Living Water
John 8:12:   The Light
John 6:35:   The Bread of Life
John 10:11:   The Good Shepherd
John 14:6:   The Way, the Truth,
                and the Life
John 15:5:   The Vine

Page 16 The Holy Place, Old Testament

Exodus 26:31–34
The colors of yarn used in making the Veil were blue, purple, red.
The hanging hooks were made of gold.
The Veil separated the Holy Place from the Holy of Holies.

1 Kings 8:1–5
King Solomon ordered the Ark of the Covenant brought to the Temple in Jerusalem.

2 Chronicles 3:1–17
King Solomon built the Temple on Mount Moriah.

Ezekiel 10:18; 11:23
In Ezekiel's vision, the Glory of the Lord departed from the Temple.

The Holy Place, New Testament
Hebrews 9:11–12: Jesus Christ is our High Priest.
Hebrews 10:10: We are made holy by Jesus' sacrifice.
Hebrews 10:19–22: The blood of Jesus gives believers the confidence to draw near to God.

Page 22 The Ten Commandments

3 You shall not misuse the name of the Lord your God.
5 Honor your father and your mother.
8 You shall not steal.
10 You shall not covet.
1 You shall have no other gods before me.
4 Remember the Sabbath day by keeping it holy.
7 You shall not commit adultery.
9 You shall not give false testimony.
6 You shall not murder.
2 You shall not make for yourself an idol.

Resources for In–Depth Study

✿ Life Principles for Worship from the Tabernacle, 2001, Barber, Rasnake, Shepherd, AMG Publishers, Chattanooga, TN

✿ A Woman's Heart, God's Dwelling Place, An In–Depth Study of the Old Testament Tabernacle, 1999, Beth More, Life Way Press, Nashville, TN

✿ The Tabernacle, Shadows of the Messiah, David M. Levy, 1993, Friends of Israel Gospel Ministry, Inc., Bellmawr, NJ 08099

✿ The Gospel in The Feasts of Israel, Victor Buksbazen, 1954, The Friends of Israel Gospel Ministry, Inc., West Collingwood, NJ 98107

✿ The Tabernacle of Israel, Its Structure and Symbolism, James Strong, 1987, Kregel Publications, Grand Rapids, MI 49501

✿ Christ in the Passover, Why Is This Night Different? Ceil & Moishe Rosen, 1978, Moody Bible Institute of Chicago

The Internet has several sites with information about the Tabernacle. The Internet site bibleplaces.com includes information and color photographs of a model of the Tabernacle in Timna Park in Israel.

Page 25

High Priest
- Sinner
- Sacrificed for his own sin and for the sin of the people
- Entered God's presence once a year
- Begged for forgiveness

Both
- Human
- Chosen by God
- Served as intermediary for people
- Authority on earth
- Died

Jesus
- God
- Holy
- Died and rose again
- Sacrificed for all people for all time
- Seated with God
- Had the power to forgive sin
- Sent the Holy Spirit
- Savior
- Authority in heaven and earth

Answers and Resources

SIZE: 100 cubits or 150 feet or 46 meters long by 50 cubits or 75 feet or 23 meters wide.

Page 35

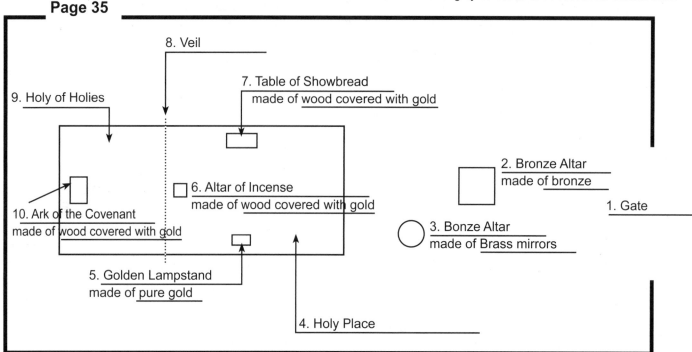

8. Veil

7. Table of Showbread
made of <u>wood covered with gold</u>

9. Holy of Holies

2. Bronze Altar
made of <u>bronze</u>

6. Altar of Incense
made of wood covered with gold

1. Gate

10. Ark of the Covenant
made of <u>wood covered with gold</u>

3. Bonze Altar
made of <u>Brass mirrors</u>

5. Golden Lampstand
made of <u>pure gold</u>

4. Holy Place

Page 35 Tabernacle Diagram

Exodus 40:34–38
When the cloud over the Tabernacle was taken up the Israelites moved onward.

Exodus 26:33–34; 40:20–21
Ark of the Testimony, also known as the Ark of the Covenant.

Hebrews 9:4
A gold jar of manna, Aaron's staff that budded, and the stone tablets of the Covenant.

God's provision, God's protection, and God's promise.

Exodus 36:8, 14, 19
Finely twisted linen, blue, purple and scarlet yarn; goat hair; ram skins dyed red, and hides of porpoises.

Blue, purple, and red.

Page 36 Tabernacle Details

Exodus 40:34–38: God's glory was seen in the cloud by day and the fire in the cloud by night.

Exodus 26:7,14: Goat hair, ram skins, hides of porpoises

Exodus 27:18:   100 cubits by 50 cubits
150 feet by 75 feet
46 meters by 23 meters

Page 36

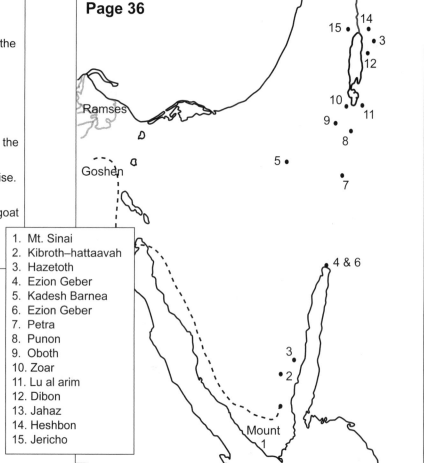

1. Mt. Sinai
2. Kibroth–hattaavah
3. Hazetoth
4. Ezion Geber
5. Kadesh Barnea
6. Ezion Geber
7. Petra
8. Punon
9. Oboth
10. Zoar
11. Lu al arim
12. Dibon
13. Jahaz
14. Heshbon
15. Jericho